THE GIRLS' WORLD
Book of Jewelry

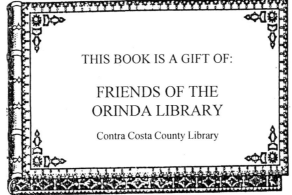

THE GIRLS' WORLD

Book of Jewelry
50 Cool Designs to Make

Rain Newcomb

LARK BOOKS

A Division of Sterling Publishing Co., Inc.
New York

This book is dedicated
to Linda Kalweit, who
taught me the right
way to make jewelry.
RN

Library of Congress Cataloging-in-Publication Data

Newcomb, Rain.
 The girls' world book of jewelry : 50 cool designs to make / Rain
Newcomb.— 1st ed.
  p. cm.
 Includes index.
 ISBN 1-57990-473-4 (pbk.)
 1. Jewelry making—Juvenile literature. I. Title.
TT212.N49 2004
745.594'2—dc22

2004004990

10 9 8 7 6 5 4 3 2 1

First Edition

Published by Lark Books, A Division of
Sterling Publishing Co., Inc.
387 Park Avenue South, New York, N.Y. 10016

© 2004, Lark Books

Distributed in Canada by Sterling Publishing,
c/o Canadian Manda Group, One Atlantic Ave., Suite 105
Toronto, Ontario, Canada M6K 3E7

Distributed in the U.K. by Guild of Master Craftsman Publications Ltd.,
Castle Place, 166 High Street, Lewes, East Sussex, England
BN7 1XU

Tel: (+ 44) 1273 477374, Fax: (+ 44) 1273 478606, Email: pubs@thegmc-
group.com, Web: www.gmcpublications.com

Distributed in Australia by Capricorn Link (Australia) Pty Ltd.,

P.O. Box 704, Windsor, NSW 2756 Australia

Art Director: DANA IRWIN

Photographer: SANDRA
STAMBAUGH

Senior Editor: JOE RHATIGAN

Cover Designer: BARBARA
ZARETSKY

Illustrator: OLIVIER ROLLIN

Associate Art Directors:
LANCE WILLE AND SHANNON
YOKELEY

Editorial Assistance: DELORES
GOSNELL, VERONIKA ALICE
GUNTER, ROSEMARY KAST, AND
JEFF HAMILTON

If you have questions or comments about this book, please contact:

Lark Books

67 Broadway

Asheville, NC 28801

(828) 253-0467

Manufactured in China

ISBN 1-57990-473-4

ACKNOWLEDGMENTS

Thanks to everybody who helped make this book possible:

Dana Irwin, who made this book beautiful and understandable through careful art direction, and **Sandra Stambaugh,** who took gorgeous photographs. (Thank you for the bubble bath!)

Lance Wille, for working hard on an impossible deadline (and meeting it)

Melanie Cooper, for lending us a hand (or two) with the how-to photography

Ben Reid, my late-night chauffeur and food-budgeter extraordinaire

Georgie Jaggers, Amanda Rogers, and **Chevron Bead and Trading Post** in Asheville, NC, for loaning us beads (and especially for putting them all back when we were done!)

Karen Levy, for her brilliant proofreading, and because she counted all those beads!

Irene Dean, Diana Light, Marthe Le Van, Allison Smith, Terry Taylor, and **Kathryn Temple,** for making beautiful projects for me

Olivier Rollin, who deciphered my instructions and turned them into beautiful illustrations

Veronika Alice Gunter, who always helped out and fed me lunch, too

And, as always, thanks to **Joe Rhatigan:** instruction guinea pig, senior editor, and granola-supplier.

Thanks to the wonderful girls who modeled, made jewelry, and had a good time with us: **Sarah, Pearl, Daniela, India, Lydia, Hana, Olivia, Alex, Skye, Adelyn, Oliana, Cierra, Sharnel, Lacey, Leila, Jasmine,** and **Anna.**

The Top Two Reasons Why You Should Make Your Own Jewelry

1

If you wear that trendy new store-bought bracelet, you know the girl who sits next to you in math class is going to show up tomorrow wearing the same thing.

2

A giant jewelry factory can't make jewelry as cool, interesting, and unique as YOU can!

The whole point of wearing necklaces, bracelets, and rings is to express yourself. I was 12 years old when I started making my own jewelry. Sure, I'd made the pasta necklaces with everybody else in elementary school, but a piece of pasta is a piece of pasta no matter how much marker you put on it. I wanted to make COOL jewelry: necklaces, bracelets, and rings that looked like the ones I saw in the mall, on movie stars, on my best friend's older sister, and in magazines. You know, stuff that would express my personal style—not something the five-year-old next door would wear. So I went to a bead store, picked out some green beads that caught my eye, and started making jewelry. Suddenly, everybody wanted to know where I got my jewelry—and when people found out I made it myself, everybody wanted me to make something for them, too.

A lot of the first pieces of jewelry I made broke or fell apart (or all the beads fell off while I was tying the knot), because I didn't have any idea what I was doing. I hope you'll be able to avoid a lot of similar heartbreak and frustration with the help of this book.

In *The Girls' World Book of Jewelry*, the first thing you'll find is a section on everything you need to know to make necklaces, bracelets, and more, plus some great tips and ideas for designing your own jewelry. You'll also find 50 awesome projects that will show you how to make real jewelry that you'll love to wear. There are projects that use beads, ribbon, wire, foam, and metal—but not a single pasta bead! I've also included several ways to make your own beads out of polymer clay, paper, metal, and even old pieces of sea glass.

Hey, I can make that!

The next thing you know, you'll be looking at jewelry around you, thinking, "Hey, I can make that!" And not long after that, you'll start thinking, "Hey, I can make that ... so much <u>better</u>!"

SPECIAL NOTE FOR IMPATIENT CRAFTERS

○ If you're the type of person who wants to be making your own jewelry NOW rather than reading anymore, you can do that. Pick out a project and read through all the instructions. The instructions will tell you when to look back to this section for important information.

Jewelry Making in Five Easy Steps

The next pages cover everything you need to know—from materials and tools to some basic techniques you'll be using over and over again. With this information, you'll be able to create any project in this book, plus countless creations of your own.

There's a lot of information on the following pages because there are a lot of different ways to make jewelry. But really, there are only five easy steps for making jewelry: Set up you work space; decide what you want to make; design it; put it together; put a clasp on it.

STEP ONE:
Set Up Your Work Space

Because everything you need to make jewelry is pretty tiny, you don't need a room stuffed with fancy equipment or even a permanent work space. With a shoebox, you can take your jewelry supplies and set up just about anywhere. You can work at your desk or at the kitchen table. You can even make jewelry in your lap. Just make sure that you're working in good light. Jewelry supplies are small enough—don't make them even harder to see by working in the dark!

Don't ever do bead work in your bed though, especially if you're working with beading needles (see page 79). They're easy to lose, and you'll wake up with a sharp needle buried in your flesh. Acupuncture is best left to the experts. Other than that, work wherever you want.

If you're using beads, work on top of a piece of cloth or felt. It'll keep the beads from rolling away, and you can keep the different types of beads you're using separate. You can probably find a cloth napkin, washcloth, or bandana in your house. If you put the cloth on a plate, you can easily move it should anyone decide to serve dinner while you're working at the kitchen table.

THE ONLY THINGS YOU NEED TO MAKE JEWELRY

• Good light (really—don't skip this one)
• Hard flat surface (such as a table, desk, or this book if you aren't reading it)
• Tools
• Supplies (beads and stuff)

GATHER YOUR TOOLS

When the creative juices are flowing, the last thing you want to do is search around the house for a pair of scissors. Before you start working on a project, get everything you need. The tools you'll find at a bead store are made especially for jewelry, so they're a little smaller than the same tool you'd find at a hardware store. A good tool can cost almost as much as a new CD. Before you wipe out your savings account, look around the house to see which tools you already have. I'm sure you'll be able to find a pair of scissors and a ruler. You may even be able to find a pair of wire cutters. You'll need these to cut through beading wire, trim head pins, and more.

wire cutters

Someone at your house is sure to know where a pair of needle-nosed pliers might be tucked away . This tool is great for squishing crimp beads (see page 29), opening loops, and playing with wire. The only tool you probably won't be able to find is a pair of round-nosed pliers. This tool, some-times called jeweler's pliers, can be found at bead stores. It's made especially for creating perfect loops. For gluing knots, especially in beading thread (see page 27), I use clear nail polish. Make sure you get the kind that has nylon in it—the other kind has chemicals in it that will eat through the thread!

needle-nosed pliers

round-nosed pliers

STORING STUFF

Dig out all those cool little containers you've saved for the day you find the perfect something to put in each one. Check to see whether there are any old film canisters, little candy tins, baby food jars, jam jars, or yogurt containers around the house. You can use anything with a tight-fitting lid to store leftover beads. Wind extra string around your fingers and use a rubber band or a twist tie to secure it. Put all the containers, string, and tools into a shoebox.

Tackle boxes are cool because they've got all sorts of dividers and compartments, so you can organize your bead stash to your heart's content. Don't flip over your tackle box full of beads though—the dividers don't go all the way to the top, and everything will mix together.

When you finish, clean up all the little pieces of string, wire, and beads that are lying around. Put all your leftover supplies in one place so you'll be ready for the next time inspiration hits.

TOOL TIPS

❍ If your needle-nosed pliers have **serrated jaws** (little ridges), they may leave teeth marks on your jewelry. Wrap a piece of masking tape around each jaw of the pliers. No more teeth marks!

❍ Instead of having two pairs of needle-nosed pliers and two pairs of round-nosed pliers, get one of each. You can use them together when you need two pairs of pliers.

❍ When you're buying tools, get the best tool you can afford and take good care of it.

STEP TWO:
What's It Going to Be?

Necklaces, bracelets, rings, anklets, earrings, headbands, hair ties, and more! So many choices ... so little time. But you have to figure out what you want to make—or at least, what you want to make first. Each piece of jewelry does something a little different.

A couple of stretchy bracelets will add a little kick to your favorite T-shirt and jeans. Earrings make an everyday outfit special. Anklets and toe rings are great for summertime, when you're wearing shorts and sandals. A cool headband or hair tie will quickly turn a bad hair day into a "Wow! Where did you get that?" day. One snazzy necklace will give new life to every outfit in your wardrobe. Naturally, you'll want to make EVERYTHING, but you can only do one project at a time. So pick one.

STILL CAN'T DECIDE WHAT TO MAKE?

If you're having trouble deciding on a first project, make a bracelet. Bracelets are a nice first project because they take just the right amount of time to make. (If you don't wear bracelets, make your first project for someone who does.)

CALCULATING MEASUREMENTS

Once you figure out what you want to make first, decide how long it will be. There are standard measurements for necklace lengths, bracelets, and anklets. You can use these if you're making a gift or if you want to sell your jewelry. Subtract the size of the clasp you use from the final measurement, otherwise your jewelry will be a little bit bigger than you thought it would be. So, if you're making a choker that's 15 inches long and your clasp is $3/4$ inch long, you'll need to bead $14 1/4$ inches before adding the clasp.

When you're making your first few projects, make sure you cut at least 12 inches more thread than you need. You'll use the extra thread for tying knots or attaching crimp beads. After you've made a few things, you'll have a better handle on how much thread you need to finish a project. Remember, you can always trim off excess thread, but you can't add thread if you don't have enough.

AMAZING MEASURING TRICK

Wrap a piece of string around your neck, wrist, finger, toe, or ankle. Drape the string to where you want the piece of jewelry to fall. (If you're measuring a necklace on yourself, use a mirror.) Mark where the ends of the string meet with your fingers, take the string off, and measure the length of the string with a ruler. Tah-dah!

Standard Measurements

Chokers: 15 inches long

Princess length: 18 inches long

Matinee length: 20 to 24 inches long

Bracelets: $6 1/2$ to 8 inches long

Anklets: 9 to 13 inches long

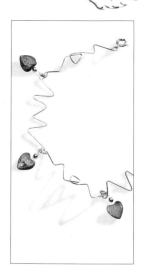

What Will It Look Like?

This is the best step because it'll really show off your creativity and style. Maybe you want your project to match your favorite dress, express your mood, or show off your style. There are two different parts to this step: the design and the beads you use to make it. If you want to start with the beads, see page 21.

DESIGN IT!

Color, pattern, and texture are the three main components of jewelry design. Some basic guidelines and hints for how to work with these elements are included in the next few pages.

WHAT? ME— AN ARTIST?

◐ If you're completely intimidated by design, don't worry about it. Everybody starts out that way. Flip through the projects in this book and pick out one you like. As you make it, think about what you like about the project. Is it the color? The way the beads fit together? When you're finished, make the project again, but change just one thing about it (such as using a different color, shape, or size bead) and see what happens. Then come back to this section and give it a whirl. The more you practice designing, the easier it gets.

Color

Color is usually the biggest part of your design. It's hard to resist the urge to use your favorite colors over and over again (most of my jewelry is green and blue). Your jewelry will look better and match more of your clothes if you experiment with lots of different color combinations.

Ideas for color combinations are everywhere. You can use the colors you see in a sunset, a flower garden, pictures from a magazine, or even your favorite shirt for inspiration. Pick out the colors that you like in the combination (you don't have to use them all) and find some beads!

You can also use a color wheel. Pick a color and put your finger on it. Here are different ways to combine it with other colors:

• Draw a line to the opposite side of the color wheel (see figure 1). This is the *complementary color*. These two colors used together will pop, creating a vivid piece of jewelry.

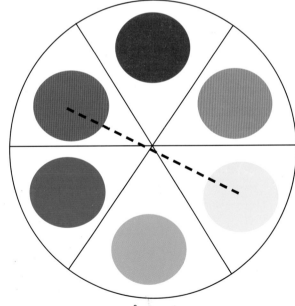

figure 1

• Draw a triangle with your finger (see figure 2 on the next page). Each corner of the triangle will point to one color. These three colors make a *triadic color scheme*. They work together the same way complementary colors do.

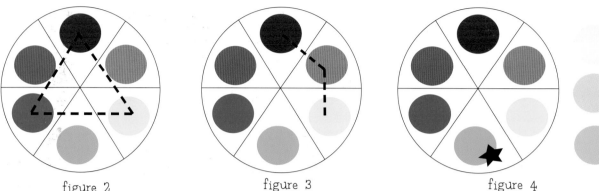

figure 2   figure 3   figure 4

• Draw a line to the colors on each side (see figure 3). This is called an *adjacent* or *analogous color scheme*. These three colors look classic and sophisticated together.

• Keep you finger where it is. Pick out multiple shades of that color and use them (see figure 4). These are *monochromatic colors*. Multiple shades of the same color look elegant and subtle.

Pattern

After you've found the perfect colors for your project, you can decide the order in which to string the colors. There are about a million different possibilities for patterns out there, and making the same pattern with different beads or even different colors can give it a whole new look. There are two ways to lay out your pattern.

1 Get all your stuff together, put it on a table in front of you, and put things together until you like what you see. (If you put everything on a piece of cloth, the beads won't roll away.) Then string the necklace, bracelet, or anklet.

2 String the beads you think will look good together. Stop after you string a few inches and see whether you like it. If you don't, take off the beads and try something different. Keep stringing and unstringing until you like what you have. Then finish the project.

If you find yourself getting frustrated because you're not happy with anything you've tried, arrange a couple of the different ideas you've discarded on your work space. Then take a break. Walk away from your project for a little while and don't think about it. When you come back to it, you'll see some new possibilities.

Here are just a few ideas for how to make patterns:

• Alternate two different beads.

• Make a unit of beads and repeat it.

• Break up units of beads with different things in between.

• Make the units bigger and smaller.

• Mix the beads together in a bowl and string them randomly.

• Make a symmetrical design (both halves match).

• Make an asymmetrical design (the sides don't match).

• Use one special really cool bead in the center.

• Put bigger beads toward the center.

• Echo the pattern you strung in the center on either side. (You can do the exact same thing you did in the center—or something a little different—on either side.)

• Let the cord show through.

(More about design on page 20.)

HOW DO YOU DECIDE WHAT LOOKS GOOD?

◐ The first thing I do is stand on my chair. Try it. Most people looking at your jewelry are farther away from it than you, and it looks different from way over there. Close your eyes and imagine you're seeing some random piece of jewelry in a magazine. Do you like it? Would you wear it? Do you think, "Hey, I want one of those," or do you think, "Ugh! What is the fashion world thinking these days?"

COOL MATH!

1, 1, 2, 3, 5, 8, 13, 21, 34, 55

⭘ Do these numbers look beautiful to you? Well, they should! This series of numbers can be found in seashells, sunflowers, architecture, and just about anything else that looks pretty. Each number in the series is the sum of the two numbers before it. For example: 1+1=2; 1+2=3; 2+3=5 ...etc. It's called the **Fibonacci sequence**, after the Italian mathematician who discovered it, and it's been a secret design tool of artists forever. It works best with beads that are all the same size. Anything you make using it will look as pretty as sunflowers and seashells (even though it won't look anything like either).

HERE'S HOW TO USE THE
FIBONACCI SEQUENCE TO MAKE PATTERNS

1. Start anywhere in the sequence. String that many of one color of bead.

2. Move forward or backward to the next number in the sequence. String that number of the second color.

3. Continue moving in the same direction, alternating two or more colors of beads, until you've gone as far as you want. Break off the sequence at any point.

4. You can repeat the unit you just strung, go backward in the sequence, or even start in an entirely different place in the sequence.

You can also make up your own "Fibonacci-esque" sequence. Pick a number. If you pick 3, add it to itself: 3+3=6. Add 6 to the number before it: 6+3=9. Add 9 to the number before it: 9+6=15. Keep adding until you're tired of it. Your sequence will be the sums of all the numbers: 3, 3, 6, 9, 15, 21, 36, etc. Use it like the Fibonacci sequence. Whatever you make will look good!

The Fire Choker uses the Fibonacci sequence for the color changes.

Texture

Texture is how jewelry looks and feels when you wear it. Texture is created by the shapes of the beads. Experiment with different shapes to get different textures. Here are some ideas:

• Put a big round bead between two rondels.

• Try barrel beads and square beads together.

• Use long skinny beads with round fat beads.

• Use different-sized beads of the same shape to create a smooth texture.

• Mix up some triangle-shaped beads with anything.

• Use seed beads between bigger beads.

• Beads with sharp edges will dig into your neck, especially if the necklace is heavy or tight fitting. Use smooth beads in the back and wherever it will rub against your skin.

Beads

The sheer number of choices of what you can use to make jewelry can be a little overwhelming at first. Beads, ribbon, foam, wire, and polymer clay are just a few of your options. Most jewelry is made out of beads, so that's what this section talks about. With a little bit of imagination, though, you can make jewelry from just about anything!

Just walk into a bead store and you'll find yourself surrounded by glittering, sparkly gems; cool, smooth beads; chunky, shiny stuff; and everything in between.

I recommend buying your beads at a bead store for two reasons. First (and most obviously), the beads there are a lot cooler than the beads at the craft store, and you've got about a million more choices. Second, the people who work at the bead store know a lot about beads. If you have any questions at all—from "Hey, do these pink and orange beads look good together?" to "How do I get this amazing bead on my necklace?"—they'll be able to help you.

Bead Sizes

The beads you find in bead stores come in all sorts of different shapes, sizes, and colors. The smaller beads, called *seed beads,* have a special numbering system. The higher the number, the smaller the bead is. Size 11° (which you say "eleven-oh") are the most common. Seed beads also come in different shapes, colors, and finishes.

Types of Seed Beads

Transparent beads will let light shine through.

Opaque beads won't let any light through.

Matte beads are etched so the surface looks frosted. They can be transparent or opaque.

Color-lined beads have a darker color painted in the hole of the bead. If you get them wet, the color on the inside will come out.

The white part of **satin** beads glows in the light.

Be careful with cheap **metallic** beads, because the finish will wear off eventually.

Triangle and **cube** seed beads come in different sizes and colors.

The larger beads are measured in millimeters. They can be made out of glass, bone, metal, stone, wood, clay, resin, and plastic. They come in a lot of different shapes and sizes. Here are just a couple of the beads you'll be seeing over and over in this book:

Tube beads are longer than they are wide, and are the same width all the way across.

Barrel beads are also long, but they are wider in the middle than at the ends.

Faceted beads have flat planes cut into them, so they catch the light and sparkle. They can be any shape.

Rondels are wider than they are high. They look like little discs.

Teardrops are narrow on one end and wider at the other.

Cube beads are square in every direction. **Square** beads are flattened lengthwise.

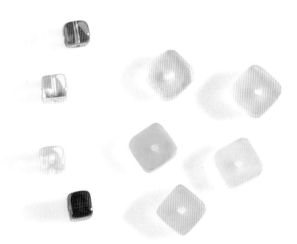

Pony beads look like gigantic seed beads.

Spacers have more than one hole in them.

Bow-tie beads look are skinnier in the middle than at the ends. The hole goes through the center.

Some beads have holes that run *vertically* (see figure 5), and some have holes that run *horizontally* (see figure 6). To make a bead with a vertical hole hang correctly, you can use a head pin or an eye pin (see next page).

figure 5

figure 6

HEAD PINS AND EYE PINS

A head pin is a small piece of wire that looks like a nail. An eye pin ends in a loop, like an eye. They're used to make earrings, hang beads, and link necklaces. You'll use a round-nosed pliers to make the loop at the top that will hold the beads in place. Once you get good at making loops, you can make your own eye pins out of wire.

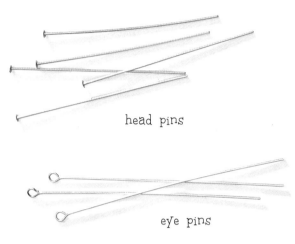

head pins

eye pins

1 Put the bead (or beads) on the head pin.

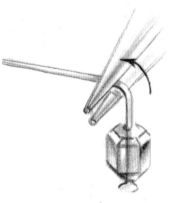

figure 7

2 Hold the wire with a pair of round-nosed pliers about ¼ inch above where you want the **bottom** of the loop to be. Bend the top part of the wire over one of the pliers' jaws, forming a right angle (see figure 7).

figure 8

3 Bend the wire down until it is doubled back on itself. Open the pliers just enough to turn them, bending the wire into a loop (see figure 8).

4 Trim the leftover wire with a pair of wire cutters.

To string the head pin onto your necklace, just thread it through the loop. If you want to attach the head pin to something (such as an earring wire), open the loop you made the same way you open a jump ring (see page 25).

You can make a loop with needle-nosed pliers, if that's all you have. It won't be very round or very pretty, but it will work. Don't try to bend wire with your fingers. You'll just end up with sore fingers and a big mess.

Make fringe with head pins. See page 56.

CHARMS AND JUMP RINGS

Charms come in all sorts of fun shapes, from roller blades to avocados to unicorns. There's nothing better than finding the perfect charm for your best friend. The only problem is that if you just string one on your necklace, it'll lay sideways so you can't see it. That's where jump rings come in.

A jump ring is a small wire circle with an opening along its circumference. If you put a charm on one, then string the jump ring onto your necklace, the charm will lay flat. Jump rings are also used to attach clasps. You need two pairs of needle-nosed pliers to twist the ring open. If your fingers are strong enough, you can use them in place of one of the pairs of pliers.

1 Hold the wire on each side of the opening with each pair of pliers.

2 Move the pliers in opposite directions (see figure 9).

3 Put whatever you want on the jump ring.

4 To close the jump ring, grasp the ends with the pliers and twist it shut the same way you opened it (see figure 10).

Never open a jump ring by pulling the ends apart. It'll never close again.

charms

jump rings

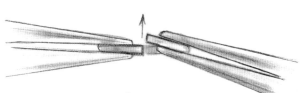

figure 9

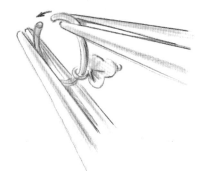

figure 10

4

Decide What to String It On

After you've picked out everything you want to make your jewelry out of and decided how you want it to go, you have to figure out how to hold it all together. Usually, this involves using some sort of thread.

There are two questions to ask yourself when picking the best stringing material for your projects: Will it fit through all the beads? Is it strong enough to hold the weight of the necklace?

Here are just a few of the more popular types of thread you'll find at a bead store. There are a lot of other options out there. Don't be afraid to experiment with new materials!

Stringing Material	Diameter (Width) from thinnest to thickest	What It's Good For	What It's Not Good For	Hints and Tips
Beading thread (single-strand nylon thread, available in many colors)	0 A B D F	Seed beads; small light beads; beadweaving; making fringe	Big, heavy beads; beads with rough edges and holes	You can do just about anything with size D. See threading tips on page 79.
Nylon-coated beading wire	The higher the number, the thicker the wire.	Large, heavy beads; medium-weight beads; beads with rough holes and sharp edges	Tying knots	Always use crimp beads with beading wire. You can use size .015 or .018 for every project in this book.
Elastic thread	0.5mm 1mm 2mm	Making projects without clasps	Large, heavy beads (they'll just stretch it out)	Always tie the ends of elastic together with a square knot (see page 31).
Illusion cord	0.010 in. 0.25mm 0.35mm	Using just a few really cool beads—the cord itself is invisible when you wear it.	Projects where the cord won't show at all. (It'll work. It's just a waste of illusion cord.)	Use the illusion cord available at bead stores instead of fishing line. It doesn't kink as easily and is more durable.
Silk beading cord	2 4 6 8	Knotting projects; stringing fragile beads such as pearls	Silk will stretch, so don't put heavy beads on it.	This cord comes with a needle already attached! Size 6 is the most versatile size.
Leather	0.5mm 1mm 2mm	Projects where you want some cord to show	Beads with small holes	Use end coils or crimp beads to finish the ends.
Memory wire (preformed coils to go around your neck, wrist, or finger)	It's all the same width.	Making jewelry without clasps	Anything you make out of memory wire will be tight and clingy.	See Chapter 2 (page 48) for lots of memory wire ideas.
Wire	32 gauge (skinny) 24 gauge (medium) 16 gauge (thick) (and many more in between)	Making loops, coils, and eye pins; hammering; wrapping beads in place	Regular stringing (the wire is too stiff)	You can get the really thin 32-gauge wire at a hardware store.

STEP FIVE:
End It

The last thing you have to do is figure out how to take your jewelry on and off. That's where clasps come in. The clasp holds the beads on the necklace and the necklace on you.

Some people like to string the entire necklace and then put the clasp on. If you want to work this way, use a piece of masking tape to hold down one end of your thread. This will keep all the beads in place when you work. Because I can never find tape when I need it, I put on one end of the clasp, string the necklace, and then put the other end on. I wrote almost all the directions in this book the way I like to do it. If you like the other way better, go for it—and don't forget where you put the tape!

To attach a clasp, you'll need to tie a knot or use a crimp bead, a bead tip, or a clamshell.

STOP!

○ When you're about to tie the last knot or squish the last crimp bead, stop and look at your project. Are there big gaps of thread showing between the beads? Is the thread pulled so tight the project isn't flexible? Fix it before you finish it.

Barrel clasps screw together. They are easy to use and generally pretty sturdy. They can catch and tear long hair.

Toggle clasps work like a button. They're good for bracelets, because you can open and close the clasp with one hand.

Spring clasps are the most inexpensive form of clasp. The spring does wear out eventually, so if you string your absolute most favorite necklace and use a spring clasp, you may need to restring your necklace some day.

Hook-and-eye clasps look exactly like they sound. If you don't mind dealing with one slightly funky end (an eye with two loops for attaching the end), sewing stores sell big boxes of them fairly inexpensively.

Lobster-claw clasps are the most stable clasp. Use them with a split ring or soldered jump ring at the other end for extra security.

Box clasps are usually made out of metal filigree, but they aren't always square. They hold together securely and are very pretty, but the "box" part is fragile.

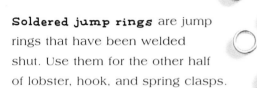

S-hook clasps are shaped like an **S** with a jump ring on each end.

Soldered jump rings are jump rings that have been welded shut. Use them for the other half of lobster, hook, and spring clasps.

Split rings are basically small key chain rings. You can use them in place of soldered jump rings or plain old jump rings.

LIGHTEN UP!

○ Make sure the clasp you pick is lighter than the necklace. If the clasp is heavier, it will always pull around to the front when you wear it.

There are several ways to attach a clasp. The kind of stringing material you use will determine which method you use. Nylon-coated beading wire attaches with crimp beads. Beading thread, silk beading cord, linen, and other things can be attached with bead tips and clamshells. Thick cord, such as leather attaches with end coils or knots. Elastic beading thread has to be knotted.

CRIMP BEADS

A crimp bead is a small metal tube that squishes around nylon-coated beading wire to hold the end of a necklace to the clasp. You'll need a pair of needle-nosed pliers, but a pair of round-nosed pliers will work in a pinch.

crimp beads

1 String the crimp bead and the clasp on the beading wire.

2 Thread the beading wire back through the crimp bead in the opposite direction.

3 Tighten the wire until the crimp bead is about $1/8$ inch away from the clasp.

4 Use the needle-nosed pliers to flatten the crimp bead around the wire (see figure 11).

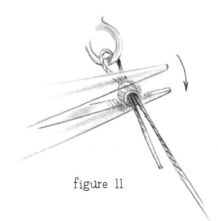

figure 11

If you become a super-duper jewelry maker and sell a lot of your jewelry, you may want to invest in a pair of crimping pliers. This tool is made just for closing crimp beads. It crushes the crimp around each wire separately, and then folds it back into a tube.

CLAMSHELLS AND BEAD TIPS

Clamshells and bead tips hide the knots in the end of a piece of jewelry and attach to the clasp. The hook at the top, which is used to attach the clasp, is usually easy to bend with a pair of needle-nosed pliers or your fingers. You can only bend it once, though—it'll break if you try to bend it again. A bead tip has a little cup that will hide the knot or a size 11° seed bead. A clamshell closes up around the knot (or seed bead).

clamshells

bead tips

1 Tie a big knot in the end of your thread or, if you're working with beading thread, around a small seed bead (see page 31).

2 Go through the bead tip, with the hook pointed toward the end of your thread (see figure 12).

figure 12

3 String whatever you want. End your project with another bead tip, as you did in step 2.

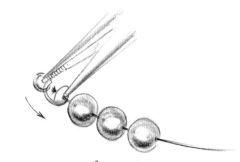

figure 13

4 Attach the clasp to the bead tips by sliding it onto the hook of the bead tip. Bend it closed with the needle-nosed pliers (see figure 13).

If you're using a clamshell, close it around the knot or bead with a pair of pliers (see figure 14) after step 2.

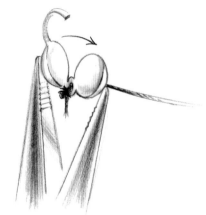

figure 14

END COILS

These pieces are used for attaching thick cord, such as leather or satin beading cord, to a clasp. To use them, dab some glue on the end of the cord and push it into the end coil. Squish the last coil around the cord with a pair of pliers.

end coil

TYING KNOTS

You can use knots to attach clasps, tie the ends of a stretchy bracelet together, or space beads apart. Keep in mind that the knot has to be bigger than the hole in the bead next to it if it's going to hold it in place, and it has to be smaller if it's going to be hidden. If you've made something that can slip on, you won't need a clasp. You do still need to hold it together, so use a square knot.

An **overhand knot** is the simplest type of knot. It can be used to tie two ends together when you're doubling thread, to make a space between beads, or to hold beads apart if you want the thread to show.

1 Make a loop in the thread.

2 Push the end of the thread through the loop (see figure 15).

figure 15

3 Pull the knot tight.

Use a **knot hidden between beads** for attaching a clasp or jump ring.

1 String the jump ring. Go back through several beads.

2 Tie a knot around the thread (see figure 16). Pull it tight.

figure 16

3 Thread it through a few more beads and trim the thread.

A **square knot** is used for ending stretchy bracelets and tying secure knots with two ends of thread.

1 Cross the two ends of thread over each other. Wrap one thread around the other (see figure 17).

figure 17

2 Pull both ends of the thread, then cross them over each other again. Wrap one thread around the other twice (see figure 18). Pull the knot tight.

3 Thread it through a few of the beads on either side of the knot and trim the excess thread.

figure 18

Tying **knots around seed beads** is good for hiding beads in clamshells and bead tips.

1 String a seed bead. Go back through the bead from the same direction, making a loop.

2 Push the thread through the loop twice (see figure 19).

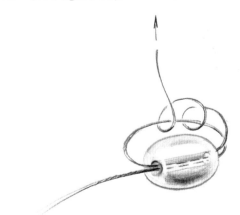

3 Pull the thread tight.

Congratulations!

You've made it to the end of the basics section. You can now make any piece of jewelry you want to. Want some ideas? Check out the rest of the book.

Before You Turn This Page...

Everything you need to know to create the 50 dazzling projects in this book is on the next pages. But what if you can't find the bead in the picture or a pair of round-nosed pliers? Read on.

"Materials" lists the beads and other supplies you'll need to make the project. If you can't find the exact bead or beads the project calls for, make a substitution. Look for something of a similar size, shape, or color. When the project you're working on calls for seed beads, it doesn't list the number of seed beads you'll need. There are two reasons for this: 1. I didn't want to count all those little tiny beads. 2. You can't buy 27 cranberry-colored seed beads (or any other specific number). Seed beads are sold in little plastic bags, in tubes, or on hanks. (A hank is a big bundle of seed beads strung on a weak cotton string.) Any one of these will give you enough seed beads to do the project AND have some left over to use for another project.

"Tools" lists all the tools you need to make the project. Remember, you can substitute round- and needle-nosed pliers for each other if you need to (see page 12). Never substitute wire cutters with a pair of scissors.

There are several projects that include instructions for making your own beads. You can use these techniques to make beads for other projects, or you can get store-bought beads to substitute for the handmade beads if you like.

You can adjust the size of anything in this book by adding more beads to make it longer or fewer to make it shorter. You can turn a bracelet into a necklace, anklet, or ring (or vice versa). Just remember to add an extra 6 inches to each end of the thread for tying knots and attaching a clasp!

Simple Stringing

Stringing beads onto thread is the most common form of making jewelry. Because there are so many different beads out there, you'll never have to make the same piece of jewelry twice. Once you do a few projects in this section, you'll be making your own variations in no time.

When you're working on the projects in this section, feel free to change the color, shape, or size of the beads you use. For example, if you love the fringed necklace on page 46 but you're morally opposed to wearing the color red, make it in blue instead.

Citrus Sparkler

Alternating two different beads is an easy way to create a fabulous necklace.

MATERIALS

54 faceted beads, 4mm (orange)

Seed beads, 11° (matte black)

2 crimp beads (silver)

Hook-and-eye clasp (silver)

Nylon-coated beading wire

TOOLS

Wire cutters

Needle-nosed pliers

WHAT YOU DO

1 Cut a 20-inch-long piece of beading wire with the wire cutters. Thread one of the crimp beads onto the beading wire. Thread one end of the clasp and go back through the crimp bead. Squish the crimp bead with the needle-nosed pliers (see page 29).

2 Thread an orange faceted bead onto the beading wire. Then string one black seed bead.

3 Repeat step 2 until you've strung 14 1/2 inches of beads.

4 String the other crimp bead and the other end of the clasp. Go back through the crimp bead and squish it. Trim the excess wire.

MATERIALS

Seed beads, 8° (black)

Seed beads, 6° (transparent amber)

26 tube beads, 8mm (animal print)

Seed beads, 10° (opal)

Seed beads, 8° (transparent yellow)

Seed beads, 10° (transparent amber)

Seed beads, 6° (black)

2 crimp beads (gold)

Lobster-claw clasp and jump ring (gold)

Nylon-coated beading wire

TOOLS

Wire cutters

Needle-nosed pliers

WHAT YOU DO

1 Cut a 40-inch-long piece of beading wire with the wire cutters. String one crimp bead and the lobster claw. Go back through the crimp bead and squish it with the needle-nosed pliers (see page 29).

2 String 3 inches of the 8° black seed beads. String a transparent amber 6° bead and an animal print bead.

3 String the pattern of beads shown in the photo.

4 Repeat step 3, stringing the same unit of beads until you've strung all the animal-print tubes. End with a transparent amber 6° bead.

5 String 3 inches of the 8° black seed beads. Add the last crimp bead and the jump ring. Go back through the crimp bead with the beading wire and squish it with the needle-nosed pliers. Trim the excess wire.

Safari Necklace

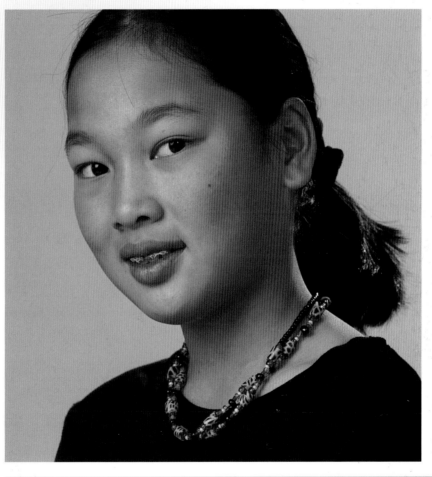

Use filler beads at the back of a necklace (such as the black seed beads in this one) to make your project the length you want it when you don't have quite enough beads.

EXPERT ADVICE

○ If you aren't sure how many filler beads you'll need, string the middle part of the necklace first (without adding the clasp). Then, string the filler beads on each side until the necklace is the length you want. When you've got exactly what you want, add the clasp. Work carefully so all the beads don't fall off!

Floating Bead Necklace

TOOLS

Scissors

Needle-nosed pliers

Stringing beads on illusion cord makes them look like they're floating around your neck. You can use crimp beads, knots, or glue to hold the beads in place.

MATERIALS

10 crimp beads (silver)

2 beads, 2.5mm (silver)

4 faceted crystal cubes, 4mm (transparent)

1 faceted crystal cube, 6mm (transparent)

Lobster-claw clasp and jump ring (silver)

Illusion cord

WHAT YOU DO

1 Cut an 18-inch-long piece of illusion cord with the scissors.

2 You'll start by making the middle of this necklace first. String one crimp bead, one 4mm cube, the 6mm cube, one 4mm cube, and another crimp bead. Center the beads on the illusion cord. Squish the crimp beads with the needle-nosed pliers (see page 29) to hold everything in place.

3 String one crimp bead, one 4mm cube, and one crimp bead on one side of the necklace. Measure 1 inch up from the center section and squish the crimp beads to hold everything in place.

4 Repeat step 3 on the other side of the necklace.

5 String one crimp bead, one silver bead, and one crimp bead on one end of the necklace. Measure 7¼ inches up from the last bead segment you added, and squish the first crimp bead to hold it in place.

6 Now you can add the clasp. String the clasp and go back through the unsquished crimp bead and silver bead. Pull on the thread to tighten it, then squish the other crimp bead. Trim the excess cord.

7 Repeat steps 5 and 6 on the other side of the necklace, attaching the jump ring at that the end.

Spiral Necklace

I t's easy to make a great-looking necklace out of a few special big beads.

WHAT YOU DO

1 Cut a 20-inch-long piece of nylon-coated beading wire with the wire cutters. String a crimp bead and one end of the toggle clasp onto the beading wire. Go back through the crimp bead with the beading wire and crush it with the needle-nosed pliers (see page 29).

2 String 2 ½ inches of seed beads.

3 String one of the polymer clay beads, and then another ½ inch of seed beads. If the holes in the beads you made are bigger than the seed beads, you may need to string more seed beads and float the spirals over them (or you could just find a larger seed bead to use).

4 Repeat step 3 until you've strung all the beads you made. Then repeat step 2.

5 String a crimp bead and the other end of the toggle clasp. Go back through the crimp bead with the beading wire and crush it. Trim the excess beading wire.

Spiral Beads

Don't like working with clay because you always end up making the same stupid snake? Well, look no further than this project: The beads are snakes with a twist!

MATERIALS

Polymer clay in several colors

TOOLS

Knitting needle

Cookie sheet

Oven

Oven mitts

WHAT YOU DO

1 To condition the clay, squeeze the piece you are going to use until you can roll it into a snake between your hands. Fold the snake in half, and roll it out again. Do this until the clay stretches (instead of breaking) when you pull the ends. Repeat this step for every color you will use.

2 Roll each color into a thin snake. Stack the snakes together and press them gently so they stick (see photo 1). With your hands, roll this thick, multi-colored snake on your work surface until it's smooth. As you roll it, it'll get longer.

3 Hold onto either end of the snake and twist so the colors spiral around the outside (see

photo 2). Don't twist it too much, or the colors will blend together!

4 Roll the new snake until it's about $1/8$ or $1/4$ inch wide. If the ends start to flop around too much, cut the snake into shorter sections that are easier to work with.

5 Cut the snake into equal-sized pieces and roll each one until it is about 2 inches long.

6 Taper the ends of each snake by applying a little pressure with your fingertips as you roll the ends against your work surface.

7 Wind each mini-snake around the knitting needle (see photo 3). You can press the clay against itself as you roll or leave some space—it depends on whether you want the cord to be visible. If you're making beads for the project on page 39, press the coils together. If you're making beads for the project on page 112, leave some space in between the coils.

8 Make sure the end of each mini-snake touches the clay in another place, so that there is a closed loop on the end of each bead. (If the ends of the beads

are open, they'll twist right off the necklace.)

9 Leave the beads on the knitting needle or skewer and place them on the cookie sheet. Bake them for 30 minutes, following the manufacturer's instructions. Remove the cookie sheet from the oven with the oven mitts. Let them cool completely before you take them off the knitting needle or skewer.

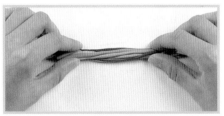

photo 1

photo 2

photo 3

Ice Blue Matinee

Pearls (and other beads) are often sold in graduated strands. The beads on the ends of the strand are small and gradually get larger toward the middle. Leave the beads on the strand and pull them off one at a time to string them.

MATERIALS

Strand of graduated white glass pearls

84 daisy-shaped rondels (light blue)

60 round beads, 1mm (silver)

2 crimp beads (silver)

Toggle clasp (silver)

Nylon-coated beading wire

TOOLS

Wire cutters

Needle-nosed pliers

WHAT YOU DO

1 Cut a 26-inch-long piece of beading wire with the wire cutters. String one crimp bead and one end of the toggle clasp. Go back through the crimp bead with the beading wire and squish it with the needle-nosed pliers (see page 29).

2 Thread the smallest white bead onto the beading wire. Add one of the daisy-shaped rondels. Continue alternating a white bead and a rondel until you've strung 5 1/2 inches of beads.

3 String one of the silver beads, a rondel, another silver bead, and the next white bead. Continue this pattern until you've strung 3 inches.

4 String an alternating pattern of three silver beads and two rondels. Then add the next white bead.

5 Repeat step 4 once.

6 String an alternating pattern of four silver beads and three rondels before adding the next white bead.

7 String an alternating pattern of five silver beads and four rondels. Add the next white bead.

8 If the bead you just added is not the largest bead on your strand, remove the beads until you get to the bead that's just a little bit smaller than the bead you just put on. Put the extra beads aside to use in another project.

9 Repeat in order steps 7, 6, 4 (twice), 3, and 2.

10 String one crimp bead and the other end of the toggle clasp. Go back through the crimp bead with the beading wire and squish it. Trim the excess wire.

Faux Turquoise Polymer Clay

This technique will show you how to make "turquoise" beads out of polymer clay. If you like doing it, try making your own "turquoise" beads for the project on page 56.

MATERIALS

1 ounce polymer clay (turquoise)

Acrylic paint (brown)

TOOLS

Waxed paper

Thick round marker or acrylic rolling pin*

Dried-out sponge

Craft knife

Template on page 120

Photocopier (optional)

Scissors (optional)

Thin knitting needle

Piece of paper

Cookie sheet

Oven

Oven mitts

Stiff paintbrush (optional)

Paper towels

*Available in the polymer clay section of craft stores

WHAT YOU DO

1 Condition the clay (see step 1 on page 40).

2 Roll the clay into a ball, then make the ball into an egg-shape.

3 Place the clay on a piece of waxed paper on your work surface and flatten it slightly with your hands. Then use the marker or acrylic rod to flatten it evenly until it's about $3/8$ to $1/2$ inch thick.

4 Press the sponge into the surface of the clay to give it texture (see photo 1). Flip the clay over and texture the other side. Be careful not to press down too hard—the clay shouldn't be thinner than $1/4$ inch.

5 Use the craft knife to trim away excess clay to look like the template. If you'd like, photocopy the template, cut it out, and place it gently in the center of the clay. Then trim around it.

6 Smooth the rough edges and round the corners with your fingers. Use the sponge to apply texture to all of the newly cut surfaces.

7 Use the knitting needle to pierce a hole from between the legs to the top of the bear. Push the needle slowly and carefully, rotating it as you push. Go back through the hole from the top to smooth out the rough edges.

8 Use the clay you trimmed away to make a bead. Roll it into a ball, squish it so it's flattened, and make a hole in it with the needle. Texture the bead with the sponge.

9 Set the pendant and bead on a piece of paper on the cookie sheet and bake for 30 minutes, following the manufacturer's instructions. Remove the cookie sheet from the oven using the oven mitts. Let cool.

10 When the pendant is completely cool, squirt a little bit of brown acrylic paint on it (see photo 2), and use your fingers (or a stiff paintbrush) to smear it over the surface of the pendant (see photo 3). Make sure you get paint in every crevice.

11 Immediately wipe off the paint with the paper towel. It will stick in the crevices. (You can add more paint if you want, or rub some water in to remove a little more.)

12 Repeat steps 10 and 11 with the bead. Let the paint dry completely.

photo 1

photo 2

photo 3

Zuni Bear Pendant

A Zuni bear is a fetish (sort of like a lucky charm) made by the Zuni people in the southwestern United States. The Zuni bear supposedly gives the person wearing it strength, the ability to adapt to new circumstances, and deep thoughts.

MATERIALS

Pendant and bead from page 42

Braided cotton cord, 2mm (tan)

TOOLS

Scissors

WHAT YOU DO

1 Cut a 28-inch-long piece of braided cotton with the scissors.

2 Thread both ends through the bead and the top of the pendant.

3 Tie an overhand knot (see page 31) 2 inches from the end. Make sure the knot is big enough to hold the pendant in place.

Simple Stringing

Silk & Crystal Lariat

Loop the lariat around your neck, cross the ends, and flop one end over the other to wear it.

MATERIALS

46 crystal beads, 3mm (green)

2 teardrops with a vertical hole, 12mm (green)

10 crystal beads, 6mm (green)

Silk bead cord (green)

TOOLS

Paper clip

Scissors

WHAT YOU DO

1 Tie an overhand knot in one end of the cord (see page 31).

2 Thread a 3mm bead and make another knot very close to the bead. To get the knot right next to the bead, unbend the paper clip and s.tick the end into the knot before you tighten it. Use the paper clip to slide the knot along the cord until it's exactly where you want it. Pull the knot tight, remove the paper clip, and finish tightening the knot.

3 Add one teardrop bead and tie a knot right above it. The fat end of the teardrop should face the first bead you put on.

4 Add another 3mm bead and tie a knot right above it.

5 Leave a space about $1/4$ inch from the last knot you tied. Then tie another knot, add a 3mm bead, and tie a knot right above it.

6 Repeat step 4 until you've put four 3mm beads on the cord.

7 Leave a $1/4$-inch space, tie a knot, and string a 6mm bead. Tie a knot right above it.

8 Repeat steps 5, 6, and 7 until all of the beads except two 3mm beads and the other teardrop have been used.

9 Leave a $1/4$-inch space, make a knot, and string one 3mm bead. Make a knot on the other side. Add the last teardrop bead (with the fat end facing away from the bead you just put on) and tie a knot.

10 Finish the end with the last 3mm bead and another overhand knot. Trim the excess cord.

Red Fringed Necklace

F ringe, the red dangles on this necklace, dresses up a plain necklace.

MATERIALS

2 seed beads, 11° (any color)

Seed beads, 6° (red)

24 round beads, 2mm (gold)

22 rondels (gold)

16 faceted beads, 6mm (red)

5 faceted teardrops with a vertical hole, 12mm (red)

2 clamshells (gold)

Lobster-claw clasp and jump ring (gold)

Beading thread, size D (see page 27)

TOOLS

Beading needle, size 10 (see page 79)

Scissors

Clear nail polish with nylon (see page 11)

Round-nosed pliers

Needle-nosed pliers

WHAT YOU DO

1 Thread the needle with the beading thread. Double the thread (see figure 1) and cut a 60-inch-long piece with the scissors. If you run out of thread at any point during this project, see the instructions on page 79 to add more.

2 String one of the size 11° beads onto the beading thread. Pull it to the end and tie a knot around it (see page 31). Dab nail polish on the knot and string the clamshell so that the seed bead rests inside it (see page 30).

3 String 10 of the red seed beads, one gold bead, and 10 more red seed beads. String one rondel, one 6mm facet, and one rondel.

4 Repeat step 3.

5 String 10 red seed beads, one rondel, one 6mm facet, and one rondel.

6 To make the middle part of the necklace, string two red seed beads, one gold bead, one red seed bead, and one gold bead.

7 Repeat step 6 three times, ending with two red seed beads.

8 String one rondel, one 6mm facet, and one rondel.

9 Repeat steps 5, 3, and 4 so that both sides of necklace match.

10 String the clamshell and the last 11° seed bead. Pull on the thread to tighten it, making sure there are no gaps in the thread, and tie a knot around the seed bead. Dab nail polish on the knot to glue it.

11 Go back through the clamshell with the needle and thread. Then go through all of the beads until you reach the beginning of the middle part of the necklace. Pull the needle through the first red bead (see figure 2).

12 String the beads to make the fringe on the far left (see photo). After you've strung the gold bead on the bottom, thread the needle back through the teardrop and all the way up the fringe (see figure 2). Pull the string tight and go into the red seed bead right next to the one you started on (see figure 2).

13 Thread the needle through to the next two red seed beads that are together. Exit between them and string the next fringe (see photo). Thread the needle back through the teardrop and all the way up the fringe. Pull the string tight and go into the red seed bead right next to the one you started on.

14 Thread the needle through to the next two red seed beads. String the middle fringe. Thread the needle back through the teardrop and all the way up the fringe. Pull the string tight and go into the red seed bead right next to the one you started on.

15 Repeat in order steps 13, then step 12.

16 Tie a knot around the thread, dab some nail polish on it, and pull the needle through a few beads (see page 31). Trim the excess thread.

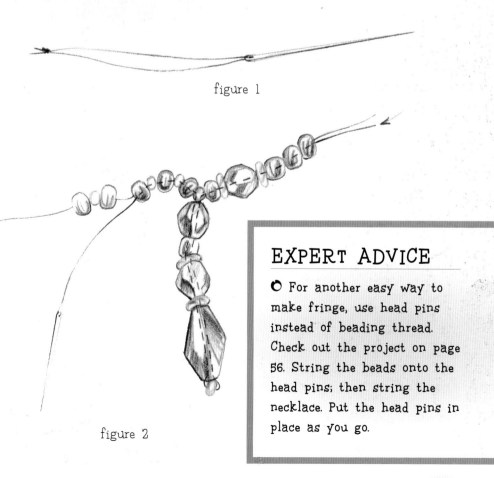

figure 1

figure 2

EXPERT ADVICE

◐ For another easy way to make fringe, use head pins instead of beading thread. Check out the project on page 56. String the beads onto the head pins; then string the necklace. Put the head pins in place as you go.

Memory Wire

Memory wire is one of the easiest ways to make a necklace, bracelet, or ring. It's a wire coil that holds its shape (hence, memory wire), so you don't need knots, clasps, crimp beads, or anything.

To measure memory wire, wrap the number of coils you want around your neck, wrist, or finger. Mark the place where the wire overlaps by 1 1/2 inches with your fingers. Break the memory wire with a pair of needle-nosed pliers there. Grasp the wire with the jaws of the pliers where you want to break it. Bend the wire back and forth until it breaks. Don't use a pair of wire cutters to cut memory wire. They aren't strong enough.

Butterfly Charm Bracelet

U se as many coils of memory wire as you want to make a bracelet that winds around and around your wrist.

MATERIALS

8 butterfly beads with a vertical hole (gold)

24 faceted beads, 6mm (champagne)

24 cube beads, 5mm (brass)

5 square resin beads, 13mm (teal)

5 square resin beads, 13mm (light green)

5 square resin beads, 13mm (yellow-green)

2 head pins (gold)

3 coils of bracelet memory wire

TOOLS

Round-nosed pliers

Wire cutters

Small bowl (optional)

Flower Power Ring

1 String a butterfly and a faceted bead onto a head pin. Make a loop in the end with the round-nosed pliers (see page 24) and trim the excess wire with the wire cutters.

2 Repeat step 1 with the other head pin. Set the head pins aside.

3 Make a loop in the end of the memory wire with the round-nosed pliers.

4 String the beads onto the memory wire randomly, until you're 1/2 inch from the end of the memory wire. You can mix the beads together in a small bowl if you like.

5 Make a loop in the end of the memory wire with the round-nosed pliers and trim the excess wire (see page 49).

6 Open one of the head pins and attach it to the loop in the end of the memory wire (see page 25). Close the head pin with the round-nosed pliers.

7 Repeat step 6 at the other end of the memory wire.

Y ou don't need to worry about sizing a ring when you make it out of memory wire. One size fits all.

MATERIALS

Seed beads, 11° (metallic rainbow purple)

Flower bead with a vertical hole (silver)

Head pin (silver)

4 coils of ring memory wire

TOOLS

Round-nosed pliers

Wire cutters

WHAT YOU DO

1 Use the round-nosed pliers to make a loop in the end of the memory wire (see page 24).

2 String the seed beads onto the memory wire. Make a loop in the end.

3 String the flower bead onto the head pin. Make a loop on the end and trim the excess wire.

4 Open the loop on the head pin and attach it to the loop on the end of the ring (see page 25). Close the loop.

EXPERT ADVICE

Make the loops turn toward the outside of the memory wire so that they won't poke into you.

Simply Marvelous Cuff

Take memory wire to a whole new level. Use a bunch of eye pins to connect two separate pieces of wire. You can also make an awesome choker with this technique.

WHAT YOU DO

1 Make sure each coil of memory wire is the same length. Set the memory wire aside.

2 String 10 purple beads onto an eye pin. Make a loop on the end of the eye pin with the round-nosed pliers and trim the excess wire (see page 24).

3 Repeat step 2 until you've made 22 beaded eye pins.

4 String four purple beads, one of the copper flowers, and four more purple beads onto an eye pin. Use the round-nosed pliers to make a loop in the end. Trim the excess wire.

5 Repeat step 4 until you've made three eye pins with copper flowers. You should have four leftover eye pins.

6 Make a loop in one end of the memory wire. Do the same with the other piece of memory wire.

7 String two purple beads onto each piece of memory wire. Slide a plain beaded eye pin onto both pieces of memory wire, connecting the two.

8 Repeat step 7 until you've strung eight plain eye pins. Add two more purple beads and a flower eye pin.

9 String three plain eye pins onto the bracelet (with two purple beads between each one), and add another flower eye pin. String three plain eye pins onto the bracelet and the last flower eye pin.

10 String the last eight plain eye pins, alternat-ing them with two purple beads. Use the round-nosed pliers to make loops in the ends of both pieces of memory wire. Trim the excess wire (see page 49).

11 String two purple beads onto one of the leftover eye pins. Make a loop just above the beads. Trim the excess wire.

12 Repeat step 11 until you've made four eye pins.

13 Open the loop in the eye pin with the needle-nosed pliers. Attach it to a loop in the memory wire (see page 25). Close the loop in the eye pin.

14 Repeat step 13 with the rest of the eye pins.

Fire Choker

Y ou can also make this necklace in shades of purple and blue for water, green and brown for earth, or white and yellow for air.

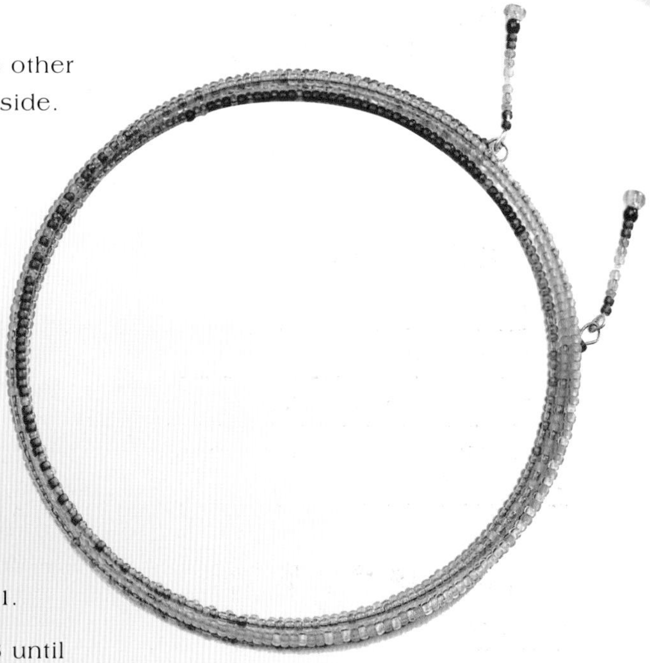

MATERIALS

Seed beads, 11° (red, orange, and yellow in as many different shades and finishes as you want)

2 head pins, 2 inches long (silver)

4 or 5 coils of necklace memory wire

TOOLS

Round-nosed pliers

Wire cutters

WHAT YOU DO

1 Arrange your beads so that they go from red to orange to yellow. If you have multiple shades of one color, arrange them from dark to light. To make this necklace, you'll string beads in red, orange, yellow, orange, red.

2 On a head pin, string two beads of each color in the same pattern you arranged in Step 1 (red, orange, yellow, orange, red). Make a loop in the end of the head pin with the round-nosed pliers (see page 24) and trim the excess wire with the wire cutters.

3 Repeat step 2 on the other head pin. Set them aside.

4 Make a loop in one end of the memory wire with the round-nosed pliers.

5 String 13 red 11° beads onto the memory wire.

6 To change to the next color (either a lighter shade of red or the darkest orange), string the beads according to figure 1.

7 Repeat steps 5 and 6 until you've strung one section of each color.

8 After you string the lightest shade of yellow that you have, string the colors in the reverse order. For example, if you strung red, orange, yellow, and pale yellow, you'll now string yellow, then orange, and then red after completing the pale-yellow section. Use the illustration to help you with the color change sections.

9 When you reach the end of the memory wire, use the round-nosed pliers to make a loop in the end. Trim the excess wire (see page 49).

10 Open the loop in one of the head pins and attach it to the loop in the end of the memory wire (see page 25). Close the loop.

11 Repeat step 10 on the other end of the necklace.

figure 1

Sea Glass Charms

Don't limit yourself to sea glass charms! You can make beads out of smooth river stones, marbles, coins, and anything else you can find using this technique.

MATERIALS

Piece of sea glass*

Jump ring (silver)

Self-adhesive foil tape (silver)**

TOOLS

Scissors

*If you don't live near a beach, you can usually find sea glass at craft stores.

**Available in the wiring or duct tape aisles of home improvement stores

WHAT YOU DO

1 Cut a ⁵⁄₈-inch-long strip of the foil tape with the scissors. It should be long enough to wrap around the outside of a piece of sea glass with about a ¹⁄₄ inch of overlap.

2 Thread a jump ring and center it on the tape. Make sure the opening in the jump ring is facing up so it won't get sealed underneath the tape.

3 Peel the backing off the tape and position the jump ring at the top of the sea glass.

4 Wrap the tape around the sea glass, overlapping the ends. Use your fingernail to rub along the tape, removing any air bubbles or wrinkles.

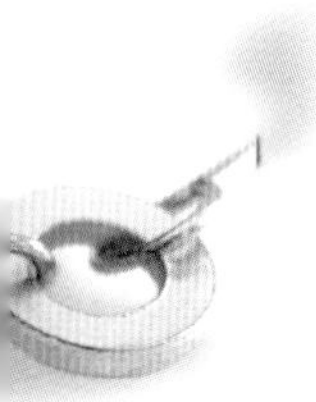

Sea Glass Dangles

Make the charming dangles on the end of this aquatic bracelet out of sea glass from the beach.

MATERIALS

2 sea glass charms from page 54

10 pony beads (matte light blue and white)

Seed beads, 11° (light blue)

Seed beads, 11° (light green)

Cube seed beads, 4mm (clear)

Tubes, 2.5mm (satin blue)

Seed beads, 6° (matte white)

12 round beads, 3mm (silver)

4 coils of bracelet memory wire

TOOLS

Round-nosed pliers

Small bowl (optional)

Wire cutters

WHAT YOU DO

1 Use the round-nosed pliers to make a loop in one end of the memory wire (see page 24).

2 String the beads onto the memory wire randomly, until you're 1/2 inch from the end of the memory wire. You can mix the beads together in a small bowl if you like.

3 Make a loop in the end of the memory wire.

4 Open the jump rings on the sea glass beads and attach each one to a loop of memory wire (see page 25). Close the jump rings.

Shooting Star Fringe

The best thing about this project is you don't have to tell anyone how incredibly simple it is to make fringe with head pins!

WHAT YOU DO

1 On one head pin, string the beads for the far left fringe (see photo). Use the round-nosed pliers to make a loop in the end (see page 24) and trim the excess wire with the wire cutters. Make another head pin exactly like this.

2 String the beads for the next fringe onto a head pin (see photo). Make a loop in the end and trim the excess wire. Make another head pin exactly like this.

3 String the beads for the next fringe onto a head pin (see photo). Make a loop in the end and trim the excess wire. Make another head pin exactly like this.

4 String the beads for the middle fringe onto a head pin (see photo). Make a loop in the end and trim the excess wire. Set all the head pins aside.

5 Make a loop in one end of the memory wire with the round-nosed pliers.

6 String one silver bead, one hematite bead, one star, one hematite, and one silver bead.

7 String 21 turquoise seed beads, one silver bead, and 21 more turquoise seed beads.

8 Repeat the pattern from step 6.

9 String 21 more turquoise seed beads.

10 String the middle part of the necklace, adding the head pins as if they were beads (see photo).

11 Repeat step 9, step 6, step 7, and step 6 so that the sides of the necklace match.

12 Make a loop in the end of the memory wire and trim the excess wire (see page 49).

Stretchy Jewelry

For jewelry that really snaps, string it on elastic! You can make hundreds of stretchy bracelets, rings, anklets, and necklaces. Make a headband or two. Use the thinnest kind to string a whole bunch of seed-bead bracelets to wear at once. Use the thicker kind to string sparkling faceted beads. (Be careful about using really heavy beads on elastic— it'll just stretch out.) Elastic beading cord is now available at every bead store and most craft stores. Don't use regular sewing elastic, because it doesn't hold up to wear and tear as well as beading elastic does.

Stretchy jewelry is great because you don't need to use a clasp to take it on and off. Use a square knot (see page 31) to close the ends. Be careful not to stretch out the elastic when you're tightening the knot. You can add a dab of glue to the knot if you like.

Jeweled Rings

Wrap your fingers and toes in sparkling crystal beads. (But don't try to put shoes on over the toe rings—ouch!)

MATERIALS

Seed beads, 8°

1 faceted bead

Beading elastic, 0.5mm

TOOLS

Scissors

Masking tape

WHAT YOU DO

1 Cut a 7-inch-long piece of beading elastic with the scissors. Put a piece of masking tape on one end.

2 String 10 seed beads onto the elastic. Add the faceted bead and a few more seed beads.

3 Wrap the ring around your toe to measure it. It should be snug enough to stay on without flopping around, but not so tight that it stretches out the elastic. Add or remove seed beads until it fits.

4 Cut the masking tape off the end of the elastic. Tie a square knot with the ends of the elastic (see page 31) and trim the excess.

Safety Pin Bracelet

Who would have thought something so dazzling could be made out of safety pins!?

MATERIALS

Seed beads, 11° (red, orange, yellow, green, blue, and purple)

Seed beads, 6° (red, orange, yellow, green, blue, and purple)

30 safety pins

Beading elastic, 1mm (black)

TOOLS

Scissors

Masking tape

WHAT YOU DO

1 Open the safety pins and string the 11° seed beads onto them. Make five pins each of solid red, orange, yellow, green, blue, and purple.

2 Cut two 15-inch-long pieces of black beading elastic with the scissors. Put a piece of masking tape on the end of each one. Thread one piece of the elastic through the loop at the top of the first red safety pin. String a red 6° seed bead onto the elastic and an orange safety pin.

3 Repeat step 2, stringing a yellow, green, blue, and purple safety pin. Put a matching 6° bead between each one. Repeat the entire pattern until you've strung all the safety pins.

4 Take the masking tape off the other end of the elastic. Tie a square knot in the ends (see page 31) and trim the excess.

5 String the other piece of elastic through the loop in the bottom of the safety pins, adding a matching 6° bead between each one. When you've gone all the way around the bracelet, repeat step 4.

YOU DECIDE

❍ If you don't like the way safety pins look, you can use eye pins instead (see project on page 52).

Hair Bands

There are all sorts of great ways to add beads to your hair! Here are several variations, all of which have been thoroughly tested to make sure they won't tear out your hair.

Splitting Hair Band

Technically, only the beads on the end of this hair band will split, not your hair.

MATERIALS

Seed beads, 8° (transparent green)

4 pony beads (blue-green)

3 washers, the same size as the pony beads

Seed beads, 8° (matte rainbow cobalt blue)

4 tube beads, 3mm (aqua satin)

Hair elastic (black)

Waxed linen (black)

TOOLS

Scissors

WHAT YOU DO

1 Cut a 7-inch-long piece of waxed linen with the scissors. Fold it in half and wrap it around the hair elastic.

2 Thread both ends of the linen through two of the green seed beads. Then add a pony bead, a washer, a pony bead, a washer, a pony bead, a washer, and another pony bead.

3 Separate the ends of the linen. String five of the cobalt blue seed beads onto on end. Add two of the satin tubes. Tie a knot in the end, as close to the last bead as possible (see page 31).

4 Repeat step 3 on the other end of the linen.

Ice Princess

The cool colors of this hair band are perfect for a winter day.

MATERIALS

Seed beads, 8° (matte transparent white)

Seed beads, 8° (silver-lined transparent)

2 cube beads, 4mm (silver-lined)

2 round beads, 5mm (silver)

Hair elastic (silver)

Waxed linen (black)

TOOLS

Scissors

WHAT YOU DO

1 Cut a 7-inch-long piece of waxed linen with the scissors. Fold it in half and wrap it around the hair elastic. Tie a double knot to hold it in place (see page 31).

2 On one end of the linen, string two matte white seed beads, one cube, two matte white seed beads, one silver-lined seed bead, one matte white seed bead, one silver-lined seed bead, three matte white seed beads, one silver-lined seed bead, four matte white seed beads, one silver-lined seed

Night Out

Make as much fringe on your hair band as you want.

MATERIALS

50 bugle beads, 4mm (gunmetal gray)

3 round beads, 5mm (silver)

5 cube beads, 4mm (silver-lined)

Hair elastic (black)

Beading thread, size D (see page 27)

TOOLS

Beading needle, size 10 (see page 79)

Scissors

Clear nail polish with nylon
(see page 11)

WHAT YOU DO

1 Thread the beading needle with the beading thread (see page 79). Double the thread and cut off a 1-yard piece. Tie a big knot in the end.

2 Go through the hair elastic with the needle. Sew through the elastic several times to hold the thread in place.

3 String 10 gunmetal bugle beads and one cube bead. Go back through all of the bugle beads in the opposite direction, making a strand of fringe (see page 57). Sew through the hair elastic.

4 Repeat step 3 once.

5 String 10 gunmetal bugle beads, one silver bead, and one cube bead. Go back through the silver bead and all of the bugle beads, making a fringe. Sew through the hair elastic.

6 Repeat step 5 twice.

7 Take a few stitches into the hair elastic, then go through the base of one of the fringes. Tie a knot around one of the beads, dab some nail polish on it, and pull the needle through a few beads (see page 31). Trim the excess thread.

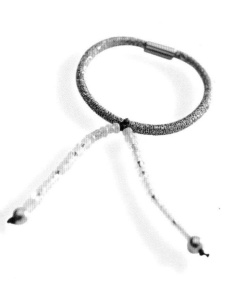

bead, two matte white seed beads and one 5mm silver bead. Tie a knot in the end of the linen, as close to the last bead as possible. Trim the excess linen.

3 Repeat step 2 on the other end of the linen.

Game Piece Beads

The game pieces in these bracelets came from old board games from Japan. If you find a game piece you really want to turn into a bead but it's plastic or too small or whatever, try using the technique on page 54. Get an adult to help you with the drilling.

MATERIALS

Wooden game pieces, 1/4 inch thick

TOOLS

Ruler

Pencil

Drill and 1/8-inch drill bit

WHAT YOU DO

1 Decide which side of the game piece you want the hole to go through.

2 Measure the side of the game piece with the ruler and divide the distance in half. Mark the halfway point with the pencil.

3 Have your adult helper drill through the game piece where you marked it.

4 Repeat for as many beads as you need.

Game Piece Bracelet

You can turn old wooden game pieces into this funky fashion statement.

MATERIALS

7 game piece beads from above

7 pony beads (red)

Beading elastic, 1mm

TOOLS

Scissors

Masking tape

WHAT YOU DO

1 Cut a 12-inch-long piece of beading elastic with the scissors. Put a piece of masking tape on one end.

2 String a red bead and a game piece. Alternate red beads and game pieces until you've used all the game pieces.

3 Cut off the piece of masking tape. Tie a square knot in the ends of the elastic (see page 31) and trim the excess.

Embroidered Headband

I f you can string a needle, you can stitch embroidery on just about any fabric.

MATERIALS

Seed beads, 11° (rainbow purple)

Seed beads, 6° (matte cobalt blue)

Black cloth headband

Beading thread, size D (see page 27)

TOOLS

Applique needle*

Clear nail polish with nylon (see page 11)

*These needles have tiny eyes and are stiff enough to go through fabric easily. You can find them at sewing or craft stores.

WHAT YOU DO

1 Thread the needle with the beading thread, double it, and cut a 1-yard piece. Tie the ends of the thread together with a big knot.

2 Go through the back of the headband where you want the first bead to go.

3 String five of the 11° seed beads onto the thread and sew into the headband so there are no gaps in the thread. Push the needle through the back of the headband, coming out between the third and fourth

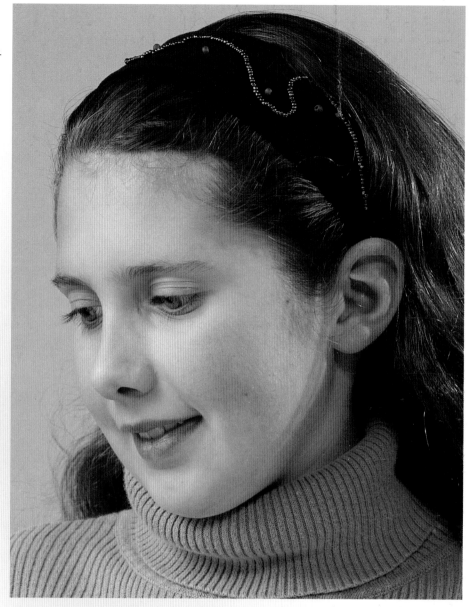

beads you just put on (see figure 1). Go through the last two beads.

4 Repeat step 3 until you've embroidered as much as you want. Add the 6° seed beads by sewing them to the headband individually.

5 Sew through the headband with several small stitches, then tie a knot on the back of the headband and dab nail polish on it to glue it.

figure 1

Multistrand Jewelry

Sometimes you've got way too many great beads to put on a single-strand necklace. That's where a necklace with lots of different strands comes in! You can make each strand a different length, or you can make them all the same. You can braid or twist the strands together, or you can let them all hang loose. Odd numbers of strands (such as three, five, or seven) look really good. Multistrand necklaces and bracelets work great with beads that are all the same size or the same color. You can also use beads of different sizes, shapes, and colors. The possibilities are endless!

Often, you'll use a special end piece called an *end cone* (see photo above) when making multistrand jewelry. The end cone attaches to the clasp and hides the ends of the strands (see figure 2 on page 71). You can find them in silver and gold. Sometimes they've got patterns in them for extra fun.

Three-Strand Rainbow Necklace

This necklace is a fun way to use up leftover seed beads from other projects.

MATERIALS

Seed beads, 5° (silver-lined purple)

Assortment of seed beads, in various sizes and colors (purple, blue, red, orange, and yellow)

2 crimp beads (silver)

Barrel clasp

Nylon-coated beading wire

TOOLS

Wire cutters

Needle-nosed pliers

WHAT YOU DO

1 Cut three 20-inch-long pieces of beading wire with the wire cutters.

2 String one crimp bead onto all three strands. String half of the barrel clasp then go back through the crimp bead. Crush the crimp bead with the needle-nosed pliers (see page 29).

3 String five of the 5° purple seed beads onto all three strands of the beading wire.

4 Organize your beads into color families. Put all the reds, oranges, and yellows in one pile. Put the blues and purples in another. If you have more than one shade of the same color, arrange them from dark to light.

5 String 1 inch of purple beads (of different colors and sizes) onto each of the three strands of beading wire.

6 String 4 inches of red, orange, and yellow beads. String the red beads first, then move to orange, then yellow, and back out again.

7 String 3 inches of purple and blue beads. Start with the purple beads, move to blue, then back to purple.

8 Repeat step 6 and step 5.

9 String five of the 5° purple seed beads onto all three strands of the beading wire.

10 String a crimp bead onto all three strands of beading wire. Go through the other end of the barrel clasp, then back through the crimp bead. Crush the crimp bead with the needle-nosed pliers and trim the excess wire.

Braided Bracelet

Y ou can braid strands of beads just like you can braid your hair. (Hey! How about braiding a strand of beads into your hair?)

MATERIALS

Seed beads, 11° (rainbow blue)

Seed beads, 6° (matte cobalt blue)

Fluted round beads, 3mm (silver)

6 faceted beads, 6mm (blue)

2 eye pins (silver)

2 small end cones (silver)

Lobster-claw clasp and jump ring (silver)

Beading thread, size D (see page 27)

TOOLS

Small bowl

Beading needle, size 10 (see page 79)

Clear nail polish with nylon (see page 11)

Safety pin

Scissors

Round-nosed pliers

Wire cutters

WHAT YOU DO

1 Mix all of the beads together, except the 6mm facets, in a small bowl.

2 Thread the beading needle with 15 inches of thread. Tie the other end of the thread to one of the eye pins (see page 31). Put a dab of nail polish on the knot.

3 Thread the safety pin through the eye pin and pin it to your work surface or a piece of cloth.

4 String 7 inches of beads from the bowl. String two of the 6mm facets, with a matte cobalt bead on either side of each one, somewhere on the strand.

5 Tie the thread to the other eye pin. Put a dab of nail polish on the knot. Tie a knot around one of the beads, dab some nail polish on it, and pull the needle through a few beads (see page 31). Trim the excess thread with the scissors.

6 Repeat steps 2 through 5 twice, making three strands of beads.

7 Braid the strands together (see figure 1). If you don't like the way it looks the first time, try it again.

8 String the eye pin through one of the end cones. Make a loop in the end with the round-nosed pliers (see figure 2) and trim the excess wire with the wire cutters.

9 Repeat step 8 on the other side of the bracelet.

10 Open the jump rings to attach the clasp to the loops in the end of the eye pins (see page 25), then close the rings.

figure 1

figure 2

Twisted Anklet

K eep this anklet clasped when you aren't wearing it to keep the twist in it. Don't use a barrel clasp with this project—the strands will untwist.

MATERIALS

Seed beads, 8° (bronze)

Bugle beads, 5mm (bronze)

25 round beads, 3mm (gold)

Seed beads, 11° (amber)

Triangle seed beads, 8° (gold)

7 faceted beads, 6mm (champagne)

2 eye pins (gold)

2 end cones (gold)

1 jump ring (gold)

Lobster-claw clasp (gold)

Beading thread, size D (see page 27)

TOOLS

Small bowl

Beading needle, size 10 (see page 79)

Clear nail polish with nylon (see page 11)

Safety pin

Scissors

Round-nosed pliers

Wire cutters

WHAT YOU DO

1 Mix all of the beads together, except the 6mm facets, in a small bowl.

2 Thread the beading needle with 18 inches of thread (see page 79). Tie the other end of the thread to one of the eye pins. Put a dab of nail polish on the knot.

3 Thread the safety pin through the eye pin and pin it to your work surface or a piece of cloth.

4 String 8 inches of beads from the bowl.

5 Tie the thread to the other eye pin. Put a dab of nail polish on the knot. Tie a knot around one of the beads, dab some nail polish on it, and pull the needle through a few beads (see page 31). Trim the excess thread with the scissors.

6 Repeat steps 2 through 5 to make another strand of beads.

7 Mix the 6mm facets into the bowl.

8 Repeat steps 2 through 5 twice, making two more strands of beads.

9 Take an eye pin in each hand and twist the strands of beads together. Twist them until they're about 7 1/2 inches long.

10 String the eye pin through one of the end cones. Make a loop in the end with the round-nosed pliers (see page 24). Trim the excess wire with the wire cutters.

11 Repeat step 10 on the other side of the anklet.

12 Open the loops you just made in the ends of the eye pins and attach the clasp and the jump ring (see page 25). Close the loops.

Chains! Chains! Chains!

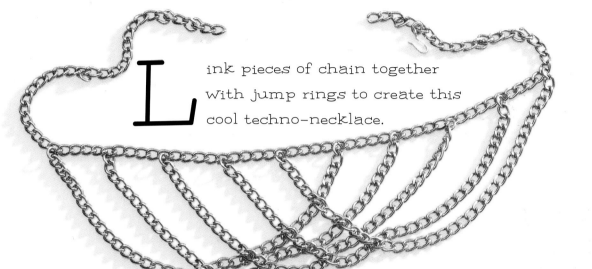

L ink pieces of chain together with jump rings to create this cool techno-necklace.

MATERIALS

12 jump rings (silver)

Hook part of a hook-and-eye clasp (silver)

58 inches of heavy chain* (silver)

TOOLS

Wire cutters

Needle-nosed pliers

Ruler

*Available at home supply stores

WHAT YOU DO

1 Cut five 7½-inch-long pieces of chain with the wire cutters. Set them aside.

2 Open a jump ring with the needle-nosed pliers (see page 25). With the ruler, measure 1 inch from the end and attach the jump ring to the chain at that spot. Add the hook and close the jump ring.

3 Put another jump ring on the chain, attaching it 3 inches from the hook. Use this jump ring to attach one of the pieces of chain you cut in step 1.

4 Use another jump ring to attach the other end of the chain 5 inches from where you attached the first end.

5 Measure 1 inch from the jump ring you put on in step 3, and attach another jump ring and another length of chain to the necklace.

6 Attach the other end of the length of chain, 5 inches from the first end.

7 Measure 1 inch from the jump ring you put on in step 5 and attach another length of chain to the necklace with a jump ring. Repeat step 6.

8 Continue adding lengths of chain to the necklace, starting each end 1 inch from the last end you put on.

9 After you've attached all five lengths of chain to the necklace, measure 3 inches from the last place a chain attaches and add the final jump ring. Trim the excess chain if you like.

Multistrand Jewelry

The Gorgeous Green Necklace

Because this necklace uses spacer beads, it's easier to string the whole thing before adding the clasp. Find that masking tape!

MATERIALS

Seed beads, 11° (transparent sea-foam green)

Tubes, 2mm (satin green)

Nine 3-hole spacers (silver)

9 crackle beads, 6mm (green)

2 extra-large crimp beads (silver)

Lobster-claw clasp (silver)

5 jump rings (silver)

Nylon-coated beading wire

TOOLS

Wire cutters

Masking tape

Needle-nosed pliers

WHAT YOU DO

1 Cut three 20-inch-long pieces of beading wire with the wire cutters. Line up the wires and put a piece of masking tape over one end of each wire.

2 String 1½ inches of seed beads onto two of the strands and 1½ inches of the tubes onto the third strand.

3 String one of the spacers. Put the strand of tubes through the middle hole of the spacer and the seed bead strands on the top and bottom.

4 String 1 inch of seed beads onto the top and bottom strands.

5 On the middle wire, string five of the tubes, one of the seed beads, and one of the 6mm beads. String one seed bead and five tubes.

6 Add the next spacer bead.

7 Repeat steps 4, 5, and 6 until you've strung all of the spacer beads.

8 String 1½ inches of seed beads onto the top and bottom strands. Tape the ends. String 1½ inches of tubes onto the middle strand. Tape the end.

9 String one of the crimp beads onto all three ends of beading wire. String the clasp, then go back through the crimp bead and squish it closed with the needle-nosed pliers (see page 24). Trim the excess wire.

10 Repeat step 9 on the other side, attaching one of the jump rings.

11 Open each of the other jump rings with the needle-nosed pliers (see page 25). Attach them to the jump ring on the necklace one at a time, making an adjuster for the clasp (see photo).

Multistrand Jewelry

Movie Star Bracelet

With this bracelet, the spacers are arranged like puzzle pieces. It might look a little tricky, but if you arrange all the spacer beads first, it's really easy.

MATERIALS

Thirty 2-hole spacers, 12mm

Seed beads, 10° (silver-lined)

Beading elastic, 0.5mm

TOOLS

Piece of cloth

Masking tape

Scissors

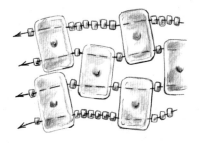

figure 1

WHAT YOU DO

1 Place the piece of cloth on your work surface. Arrange the spacers as shown in figure 1.

2 Cut a 12-inch long piece of beading elastic with the scissors. Put a piece of masking tape on one end.

3 Begin stringing the top row of beads. Thread one spacer, six seed beads, and one spacer.

4 Measure the distance between the spacers by holding one of the other spacers between them. There should be a seed bead on either side of the extra spacer. Adjust the number of seed beads so there is.

5 String the number of seed beads you just figured out (step 4) between each spacer, until all the spacers on the top row are strung.

6 Cut the masking tape off the end of the elastic. Tie a square knot in the ends (see page 31) and trim the excess with the scissors.

7 To add the second row of beads, repeat step 2. String it through the bottom hole of one of the spacers in the top row.

8 String one seed bead, one spacer, and one seed bead.

9 Repeat step 8 until all the beads on the second row are strung. Take the masking tape off and close the tie with a square knot.

10 To add the third row of beads, repeat steps 7, 8, and 9.

11 To add the fourth row of beads, go through the bottom hole of a spacer on the third row. Add the number of seed beads you figured out in step 4. Go through the next spacer.

12 Repeat step 11 until all the spacers are strung. Cut off the masking tape and tie a square knot in the ends of the elastic.

Beadweaving

Beadweaving is a way of putting beads together so they don't just lay next to each other in a long line. Generally, it's done with teeny tiny needles that go through each bead several times with thread. You can find these special needles with really small eyes in bead stores. You can use bigger beads for any of the projects in this chapter, but just make sure your thread is thin enough to go through the beads several times.

Beadweaving uses up lots of thread. You may need to add new thread before you finish your project. To do this, tie a knot around the last bead you put on (see page 31) and weave the thread through several of the surrounding beads before cutting it. Then, string a new piece of thread, go through several already-strung beads, tie a knot around one of them, and go through the last strung bead.

There are about a million different ways to weave beads together. Here are a few of them.

EXPERT ADVICE

○ To thread a beading needle, cut the beading thread at an angle with sharp scissors. Squish it flat between your fingertips. Hold it steady while you push the needle onto it. If the thread starts to fray, cut it and try again.

Totally Tubular Bracelet

This bracelet is made with the simplest version of ladder stitch. Each bead is like the rung of a ladder.

YOU DECIDE

○ If you don't want to make your own beads, try making this bracelet with long glass, wood, metal, or bone tubes. Don't use bugle beads, though—the sharp ends will cut through the elastic thread.

MATERIALS

43 vellum beads from page 82 (yellow, purple, and teal)

Elastic beading thread, 0.5mm

TOOLS

Scissors

WHAT YOU DO

1 Cut 4 yards of the elastic beading thread with the scissors. String a yellow bead and center it on the thread.

2 String a purple bead on one side of the thread. Thread the other end through the bead from the opposite direction (see figure 1). Pull both ends of the thread so that the beads fit snugly together. Be careful not to pull it too tight—you don't want the elastic to stretch.

3 Repeat step 2, stringing yellow, purple, teal, purple, yellow, teal, purple, teal, yellow until the bracelet is long enough to fit around your wrist.

4 To close the bracelet, thread both ends of the thread through the first bead you put on (just like it's another bead).

5 With one end of the thread, tie a knot (see page 31) and go through another bead. Trim the excess thread.

6 Repeat step 5 on the other end.

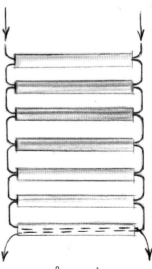

figure 1

Map Necklace

T his necklace uses paper beads made out of an old map. The map beads are woven together in a variation of ladder stitch.

MATERIALS

28 map beads from page 82

Triangle seed beads, 11° (black)

15 bow-tie beads (black)

2 clamshells (silver)

Box clasp (silver)

Beading thread, size D (see page 27)

TOOLS

Scissors

Clear nail polish with nylon (see page 11)

Needle-nosed pliers

WHAT YOU DO

1 Cut 2 yards of beading thread with the scissors. String one triangle bead and center it on the thread.

2 Thread both ends of the thread through a clamshell (see page 30) and another triangle bead.

3 Separate the threads and string three triangle beads on each side.

4 String a bow-tie bead onto one thread. Then string the other thread through the bead from the opposite direction (see figure 1).

5 String one map bead onto each thread.

6 Repeat steps 4 and 5 until you've strung all the beads, ending with a bow-tie bead.

7 String three triangle beads onto each thread. Then bring both ends through one triangle bead in the same direction.

8 Go through the clamshell, and add another triangle bead. Tie a knot around the bead, dab some nail polish on it, and pull the needle through the clamshell and a few beads (see page 31). Trim the excess thread.

9 To attach the box clasp, thread the ends of the clamshells through the loops on the clasp. Bend the end of the clamshells with the needle-nosed pliers to hold them in place (see page 30).

Paper Beads

Paper beads are really, really fun (and easy) to make, and you can create them out of any kind of paper you want.

MATERIALS

Paper (old maps or yellow, teal, and purple vellum)

Template (see page 120)

White craft glue

Water

TOOLS

Wax paper

Small bowl

Photocopier

Scissors

Pencil

Cardboard (optional)

Toothpick

Small paintbrush

WHAT YOU DO

1 Cover your work surface with the wax paper. In the small bowl, mix equal parts of the white craft glue and water.

2 Copy the template on page 120. The triangular template will make beads like the ones on page 81. The rectangular template will make beads like the ones on page 80. For an extra-sturdy template, cut around the copied template with scissors and trace it with the pencil onto a piece of cardboard.

3 Trace the template onto the back of the paper with the pencil. Cut it out.

4 Wrap the piece of paper (starting with the wide end of the base of the triangle or the shorter end of the rectangle) around the pencil (see photo 1). This will help break up the fibers in the paper and make it easier to do the next step.

5 Roll the piece of paper around the toothpick (see photo 2). If you're working with a triangle, start with the widest end.

6 Unroll about ¼ or ½ inch of the paper and brush the glue mixture onto it with the paintbrush (see photo 3). Reroll the end of the paper, slip it off the toothpick, and set it aside to dry. If you're working with vellum, run your fingernail along the seam after you glue it. This will help make it stick.

7 Repeat steps 3 through 6 for each bead you want to make. When you're finished, wash the glue out of the brush with hot soapy water. Let the beads dry overnight.

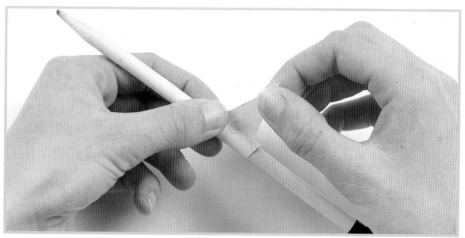

photo 1

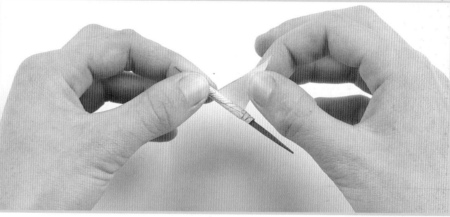

photo 2

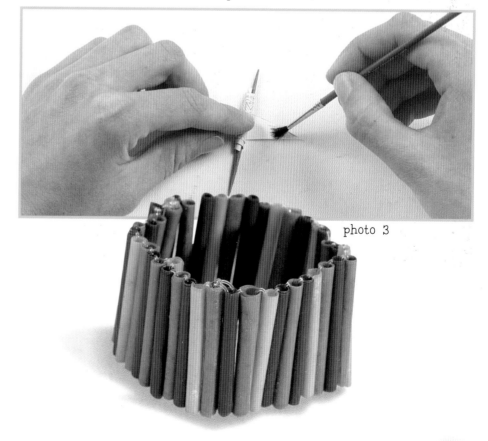

photo 3

Daisy-Chain Necklace

Daisy chain is a pretty straightforward stitch. Make a garland of flowers to hang around your neck. You can make daisy rings, headbands, and earrings, too!

MATERIALS

Seed beads, 11° (green)

Seed beads, 11° (white)

Seed beads, 11° (yellow)

Seed beads, 11° (orange)

Seed beads, 11° (purple)

2 eye pins (silver)

2 end cones (silver)

2 jump rings (silver)

S-hook clasp (silver)

Beading thread, size D (see page 27)

TOOLS

Beading needle, size 11 (see page 79)

Clear nail polish with nylon (see page 11)

Scissors

Round-nosed pliers

Wire cutters

WHAT YOU DO

1 Thread the beading needle with 1 yard of thread. Tie the other end of the thread to one of the eye pins. Put a dab of nail polish on the knot.

2 String eight green beads and six white beads. Go back through the first white bead you put on, forming a loop (see figure 1). Pull the thread tight.

3 String one yellow bead and go through the fourth white bead (see figure 1). Pull the thread tight. There should be two white beads on either side.

4 Repeat steps 2 and 3, alternating the colors of the flower petals between white, yellow, orange, and purple, until you have a strand 16 inches long.

5 Tie the thread around the other eye pin and dab some nail polish on the knot.

6 Repeat steps 2 through 5 to make two more strands of daisy chain.

7 When you've strung three strands of daisy chain, tie a knot around one of the beads (see page 31). Dab some nail polish on it, and pull the needle through a few beads. Trim the excess thread with the scissors.

figure 1

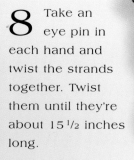

EXPERT ADVICE

❍ To practice this stitch, make a few daisies on a short piece of thread. Thread your beading needle with 8 inches of thread. String a bead and tie a knot around it (see page 31) at the end of the thread. String a few seed beads, then make a daisy. If it doesn't look anything like the ones in the picture, don't panic. It's not you—it's the thread tension. Hold the beadwork in one hand and pull on one half of the petal beads (don't pull on the bead in the center). Some of the beads will move closer together and you'll see big gaps in the thread. Pull on the needle and thread. The gaps will disappear. Practice making a few daisies. Once you've got it down, experiment with different length "stems" to vary the look of the pattern.

8 Take an eye pin in each hand and twist the strands together. Twist them until they're about 15 1/2 inches long.

9 String one of the eye pins through an end cone. Make a loop in the end of the eye pin with the round-nosed pliers (see page 24). Trim the excess wire with the wire cutters.

10 Repeat step 9 with the other eye pin.

11 Open the jump rings to attach them to the loops in the ends of the eye pins. Attach the clasp to the jump rings and close them (see page 25).

Oglala Butterfly Bracelet

Don't be fooled by how complicated this bracelet looks; it's actually quite simple. It was invented by the young women of the Oglala Lakota Nation.

MATERIALS

Seed beads, 11° (dark blue)

Seed beads, 11° (white)

Seed beads, 11° (light blue)

2 bead tips (silver)

4 jump rings (silver)

Toggle clasp (silver)

Beading thread, size D (see page 27)

TOOLS

Beading needle, size 12 (see page 79)

Clear nail polish with nylon (see page 11)

Scissors

Needle-nosed pliers

WHAT YOU DO

1 Thread the beading needle with 1 yard of thread.

2 String one dark blue bead and tie a knot around it (see page 31). Dab nail polish on the knot and pull the bead through the bead tip (see page 30).

3 String enough dark blue beads to fit around your wrist. String the other bead tip and add another dark blue bead.

4 Go back through the bead tip so that the dark blue bead you just added rests inside of it. Go through the first dark blue bead on the other side of the bead tip.

5 String three white beads. Go through the third blue bead, making a triangle of white beads in between every three dark blue beads (see figure 1).

6 Repeat step 5 along the length of the bracelet.

7 When you reach the other side of the bracelet, thread the needle through the bead tip on that end. Go through the bead tucked inside of it. Go back through the bead tip, the dark blue beads on the other side, and up through the first two white beads.

figure 1

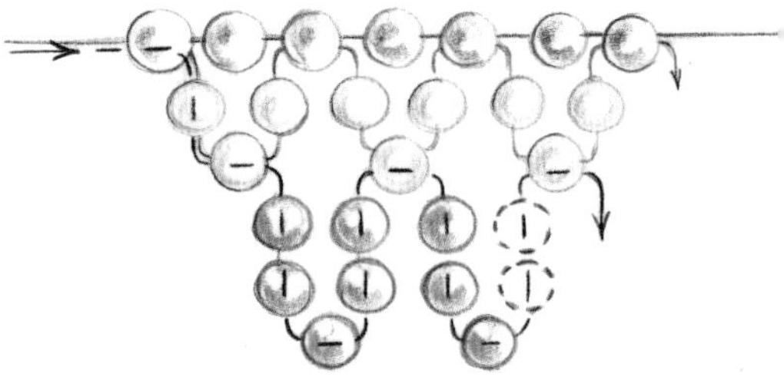

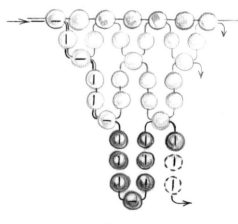

figure 2

figure 3

8 String five light blue beads and go through the middle bead on the next white triangle (see figure 2).

9 Repeat step 8 along the length of the bracelet.

10 When you reach the other side of the bracelet, repeat step 7 to turn the thread around. After you've gone through the first two white beads, thread the needle through the first three light blue beads.

11 String seven dark blue beads and go through the third light blue bead in the next section (see figure 3).

12 Repeat step 11 until you've reached the other side of the bracelet.

13 Tie a knot around one of the beads, dab some nail polish on it, and pull the needle through a few beads (see page 31). Trim the excess thread with the scissors.

14 Use the needle-nosed pliers to close the bead tips around a jump ring (see page 25).

15 Add another jump ring to each end of the bracelet and attach the toggle clasp (see page 25).

Cubed Toe Rings

Right-angle weave makes all the beads lie in a square, perpendicular to one another. You can use any kind of bead for right-angle weave.

MATERIALS

Cube seed beads, 4mm (matte orange or dark green)

Elastic beading thread, 0.5mm

TOOLS

Scissors

WHAT YOU DO

1 Cut a 12-inch-long piece of elastic thread with the scissors.

2 String four cube beads onto the thread. Go back through the first bead you put on, and pull the thread so that the beads form a square (see figure 1). Don't pull so tight that you stretch the elastic.

3 Thread through the two beads next to the bead you just went through. Add three more cube beads to the thread, and go through the last bead on the first square.

4 Repeat step 3 until the ring is almost long enough to fit around your toe. There should be a gap big enough for one more bead.

5 String one bead and go through the vertical bead in the first square you put on. Add another bead and go through the vertical bead in the last square you added. Pull the thread tight to make the final square.

6 Thread through a few more beads and tie a knot around the thread (see page 31). Pull it tight and go through a few more beads. Trim the excess thread.

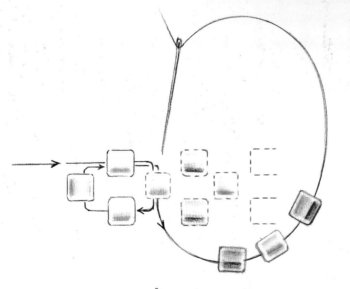

figure 1

Bodacious Barrettes

These sparkly barrettes will turn a bad hair day around in a flash.

MATERIALS

19 faceted beads, 4mm (pink, amber, or purple)

French-style barrette blank*

Wire, 34 gauge

TOOLS

Wire cutters

*Available at bead and craft stores

WHAT YOU DO

1 Cut an 18-inch-long piece of wire with the wire cutters.

2 String four beads and center them on the wire. Go back through the first bead you put on from the opposite direction, making a square (see figure 1).

3 Add two beads to one end of the wire, then one bead to the other end. With the wire that only has one bead on it, go back through the first bead on the other side, making a loop (see figure 1).

4 Repeat step 3 until you have enough beads to cover the barrette.

5 Pull both ends of the wire down around the last bead you put on. Twist them together snugly, then feed them through the hole on the end of the barrette.

6 Separate the ends of the wire and push each one through a bead on each side of the barrette.

7 Cross the wires on the underside of the barrette and repeat step 6 with the next two beads.

8 Repeat steps 6 and 7 until you've attached the beads to the entire length of the barrette.

9 Twist the ends of the wire together and push them through a bead. Trim the excess wire.

Wire Jewelry ....

You can do all sorts of stuff with wire…twist it, bend it, coil it, or hammer it. It'll keep its shape when you're through! You can make jewelry out of nothing but wire, or you can decorate the wire with beads and charms.

There are lots of ways to get wire. You can use colored craft wire—it comes in fun colors and is easy to bend and twist. Or you can flatten paper clips and use them as pieces of wire. For really fancy jewelry, you can use sterling silver or gold wire. It's a good idea to practice with cheaper wire before working with the more expensive silver or gold wire. Copper is cheap, easy to find, fun to work with, and pretty!

Sea Glass Charm Necklace

One of the best sources of wire can be found just about anywhere—paper clips!

MATERIALS

3 sea glass charms from page 54

13 washers, 5/8 inch wide (silver)

Lobster-claw clasp (silver)

6 jump rings (silver)

14 paper clips (silver)

TOOLS

Round-nosed pliers

Wire cutters

WHAT YOU DO

1 Flatten the paper clips with the round-nosed pliers and cut them into 1 3/4-inch lengths with the wire cutters.

2 Make a loop in one end of a paper clip with the round-nosed pliers (see page 24). Make a loop in the opposite direction at the other end.

3 Open the loop in one end of the paper clip with the pliers (see page 25). Attach one of the washers and close the loop.

4 Attach another washer to the other end of the paper clip, as you did in step 3.

5 Repeat steps 2, 3, and 4 with each paper clip and washer.

6 Open the loop in the last paper clip to attach the lobster-claw clasp.

7 For each of the sea glass charms, attach a jump ring to the jump ring on top. Attach another jump ring to the one you just put on.

8 Find the washer at the center of the necklace. Open the top jump ring on a sea glass charm and attach it to the washer. Close it.

9 Attach a sea glass charm to the washers on either side of the center washer, like you did in step 8.

Heart Anklet

Bend paper clips into links and add some pearl hearts for an anklet you'll want to wear all summer long.

MATERIALS

5 pearl hearts with a vertical hole (purple)

5 beads, 3mm (silver)

5 paper clips (silver)

5 head pins (silver)

Jump ring (silver)

Spring ring clasp (silver)

TOOLS

Needle-nosed pliers

Round-nosed pliers

Wire cutters

WHAT YOU DO

1 Flatten the paper clips with the needle-nosed pliers.

2 Make a loop at each end of every paper clip with the round-nosed pliers (see page 24).

3 With the needle-nosed pliers, bend angles and loops into each paper clip. They don't need to match each other—and they'll actually look better if they don't! Set the bent paper clips aside.

4 String a pearl heart onto a head pin. Add one of the silver beads and use the round-nosed pliers to make a loop in the top (see page 24).

5 Repeat step 4 with the rest of the head pins, pearls, and silver beads.

6 To attach the paper clips to each other, open the loop in one end of the first paper clip (see page 25). Thread the loop of a head pin and the loop of another paper clip onto the loop you opened. Close the loop.

7 Repeat step 6 until you've attached all the clips and head pins.

8 Open the loop on the end of the last paper clip and attach the clasp. Attach the jump ring (see page 25) to the other end of the anklet.

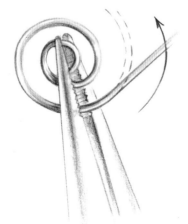

Twisty Bead Ring

This ring design makes a great gift for a friend. You don't even need to know how big to make it—it's adjustable.

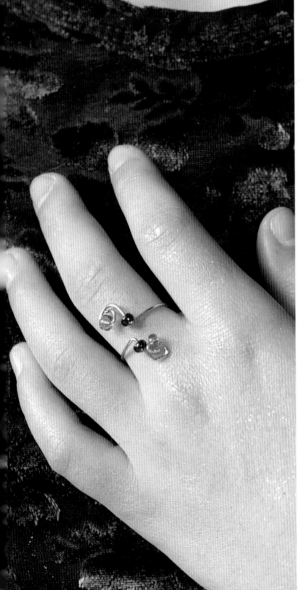

Seed beads, 6° (green)

Seed beads, 8° (blue)

Paper clip (silver)

Needle-nosed pliers

Marker (or something about the width of a finger)

WHAT YOU DO

1 Straighten out the paper clip with the needle-nosed pliers.

2 Wrap the wire around the marker. Make a right angle in each end where the wire meets. Make sure the pieces are going in opposite directions.

3 To make a spiral in one end of the wire, begin to bend the end of the wire into a loop (see page 24) but don't close it all the way. Hold the loop flat with a pair of pliers and continue to bend the wire into a spiral (see figure 1). Make it as big or as little as you want. String a blue bead and a green bead before closing the loop all the way.

4 Repeat step 3 on the other side.

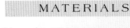

figure 1

Fancy Paper Clip Bracelet

Forget those boring silver paper clips! Look in craft and office supply stores for fancy shapes and colors. You may have to fiddle around a bit to get the bracelet to work, but it's worth the effort.

MATERIALS

Coiled wire beads (green) on page 101 (You'll need one for each paper clip link.)

Fancy rectangular paper clips*

Hook part of a hook-and-eye clasp

Jump ring (optional)

TOOLS

Needle-nosed pliers

*Available at office supply stores and in the scrapbooking section of craft stores. They're really easy to make, so if you can't find them, see page 96 for instructions.

WHAT YOU DO

1 Line up the paper clips on your work surface. Find the loose end of one paper clip. Put it at the top of the necklace. Find the loose end of the next paper clip and put it at the bottom of the necklace.

2 Repeat step 1, arranging the paper clips top to bottom, until you've laid out all of the paper clips.

3 Pick up the first two paper clips and hold them back to back. Make sure the loose ends of the paper clips are opposite each other (see figure 1).

4 Wind one of the coil beads onto both edges of the paper clip, where they will link together (see figure 1).

5 Repeat steps 3 and 4 until you've linked all of the paper clips together.

6 Wind the last coil bead onto the edge of the last paper clip. Attach the hook clasp to the coil. If you can't wind it right onto the coil, use a jump ring to attach it (see page 25).

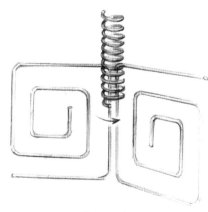

figure 1

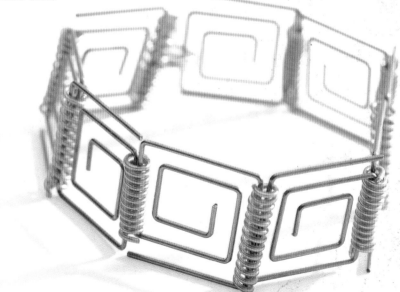

Wire Rectangle Paper Clips

If you can't find the fancy paper clips used for the project on page 95, you can easily make them yourself by bending a few right angles into a piece of wire.

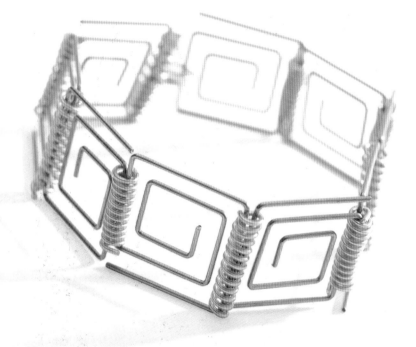

MATERIALS

Wire, 22 gauge (copper)

Template on page 120

TOOLS

Wire cutters

Needle-nosed pliers

WHAT YOU DO

1 Cut a 6½-inch-long piece of copper wire with the wire cutters.

2 Use the needle-nosed pliers to make right angles in the wire, following the template. It's easier to start with the smaller bends on the inside.

3 Trim the excess wire with the wire cutters.

4 Repeat steps 1 through 3 until you've made as many paper clips as you want.

Make a few more links to create a necklace.

Polka-Dot Necklace

F ind some long head pins to bend, bead, and twist into this dazzling necklace.

MATERIALS

14 barrels, 22mm
(green with black dots)

Seed beads, 11° (transparent green)

Lobster-claw clasp (silver)

14 head pins, 3 inches long (silver)

TOOLS

Round-nosed pliers

Wire cutters

WHAT YOU DO

1 String a barrel bead onto one of the head pins. Use the round-nosed pliers to make a loop right above it (see page 24).

2 String 13 seed beads onto the head pin. Make a loop right above the last bead and trim the excess wire with the wire cutters.

3 Repeat steps 1 and 2 until you've used all the head pins.

4 Open the loop on the end of one of the head pins and string it through the loop right above the bead on another head pin (see page 25). Close the loop. It should look like figure 1.

5 Repeat step 4 to link all the head pins.

6 Open the loop on the last head pin and attach the clasp. Close the loop.

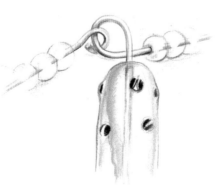

figure 1

Polka-Dot Ring

Make a matching ring for your necklace on page 97, or use this technique to make any long, skinny bead that catches your eye into a ring.

MATERIALS

2 round beads, 2.5mm (silver)

1 barrel, 22mm (green with black dots)

Paper clip (silver)

TOOLS

Needle-nosed pliers

Round marker (or something about the width of a finger)

WHAT YOU DO

1 Straighten out the paper clip with the needle-nosed pliers.

2 Wrap the wire around the marker. Cross the wires where they meet.

3 With the pliers, make a wide angle in each end of the wire. Make sure the pieces are going in opposite directions.

4 String a silver bead onto one end of the wire. Add the barrel bead and bend the wire so it's directly over the ring.

5 String a silver bead onto the other end of the wire. Shove the end of the wire through the other end of the barrel bead.

Polka-Dot Earrings

Okay, now for the matching earrings!

MATERIALS

4 round beads, 2mm (silver)

2 barrels, 22mm (green with black dots)

2 head pins, 3 inches long (silver)

TOOLS

Round-nosed pliers

WHAT YOU DO

1 String a round bead, a barrel, and a round bead onto a head pin.

2 With the round-nosed pliers, bend the head pin into a U about 1/2 inch away from the last bead.

3 Repeat steps 1 and 2 to make the other earring.

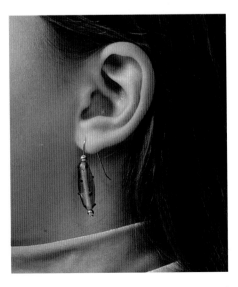

Coiled Wire Beads

ll you need to make these beads is some wire and a knitting needle.

MATERIALS

Colored craft wire, 22 gauge (green or purple and blue)

TOOLS

Wire cutters

Knitting needle

WHAT YOU DO

1 Cut a 12-inch-long piece of wire with the wire cutters.

2 Hold one end of the wire on the knitting needle with your thumb. Wind the wire around the knitting needle. Be careful not to overlap the coils, and make sure there aren't any big gaps between the coils (see figure 1).

3 When you've wound all the wire, slide it off the knitting needle. They should be about 1 inch long when you're done. If your coil bead needs to be shorter, trim the extra with the wire cutters.

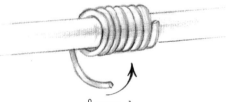

figure 1

MAKE YOUR OWN JUMP RINGS!

○ Making your own jump rings is as easy as winding wire around a knitting needle and taking it off. Position the wire cutters so that you're cutting down the top of the tube. Start cutting—you'll have a whole pile of jump rings!

Funky Wire Bracelet

This project will have you doing loopy loops in your dreams.

MATERIALS

5 coiled wire beads from page 101 (purple and blue)

Copper-coated wire, 22 gauge (purple and blue)

TOOLS

Wire cutters

Knitting needle

Round-nosed pliers

Bamboo skewer

Needle-nosed pliers

WHAT YOU DO

1 Make a loop at each end of the coil beads with the round-nosed pliers (see page 24).

2 To make the center bead, cut a 40-inch piece of the blue wire. Wind it around the bamboo skewer to make a tight, thin coil about 4 inches long.

3 Cut a 60-inch long piece of purple wire. Thread it through the middle of the blue coil. Wind the end of the purple wire around the knitting needle until you have a coil about 1-inch long. Slide the blue coil down so that it's snug against the purple coil. Continue to wind the purple wire around the knitting needle. The blue coil will twist around, making the center bead (see photo). Trim the wire and make loops in the ends.

4 Open the loop in the end of a blue coil with the pliers and attach it to one end of the center bead (see page 25). Do the same on the other side.

5 Continue to attach the coil beads together as you did in step 5.

6 To make the loop end of the clasp, cut a 1-inch piece of purple wire. Make it into a circle and squeeze it together in the middle. Cut a 1/2-inch piece of wire and wrap it around the middle of the circle, forming a figure 8. Trim the ends of the wire and attach it to the loop in one end of the bracelet.

7 To make the hook, cut a 1 1/2-inch piece of wire. Repeat step 6 to make the wire into a figure 8. Then, flatten the top half of the figure 8 and fold it over to form a hook. Trim the ends of the wire and attach it to the loop in one end of the bracelet.

Fairy Earrings

These charming little earrings glow in the dark. Adding seed beads to a jump ring is a great way to dress up a simple charm.

MATERIALS

10 round beads, 3mm (glow-in-the-dark)

2 fairy charms

2 jump rings, 6mm (silver)

2 ear wires (silver)

TOOLS

Needle-nosed pliers

WHAT YOU DO

1 Open the first jump ring with the needle-nosed pliers (see page 25).

2 String two beads, the fairy charm, three beads, and the ear wire.

3 Close the jump ring (see page 25).

4 Repeat steps 1 through 3 to make the other earring. When you add the fairy charm, make sure it's facing the opposite direction of the first fairy.

EVEN EASIER EARRINGS

◐ One of the simplest ways to make earrings is with head pins. String the beads you want onto a head pin and make a loop on the top (see page 24). Open the loop and attach it to the earring wire (see page 25). If you use an eye pin to make earrings, you can add dangles to the eye.

Squished Silver Earrings

Y ou can add beads to your hammered wire creations. Be careful where you hammer though.

MATERIALS

Seed beads, 11° (cranberry)

Seed beads, 6° (matte cobalt blue)

Wire, 24 gauge (silver)

TOOLS

Wire cutters

Piece of felt

Sidewalk

Flathead screwdriver

Hammer

Round-nosed pliers

Metal file*

*Available at bead stores

WHAT YOU DO

1 Cut two 4-inch-long pieces of wire with the wire cutters.

2 Set the wires on a piece of felt on the sidewalk.

3 Hold the end of the flathead screwdriver over the end of the first piece of wire. Hit it with the hammer. (This will hold the beads in place.)

4 Repeat step 3 with the other piece of wire.

5 Thread a cranberry and a blue bead onto one end of the wire.

6 Bend the wire with the round-nosed pliers so it snakes back and forth (see photo). Start to bend it about ³/4 inch from the hammered end. Stop bending the wire 2¹/2 inches from the end.

7 Repeat steps 5 and 6 with the other piece of wire. Bend a mirror image of the first piece of wire.

8 Set one piece of wire on a piece of felt on the side-walk. Hammer the bends with the hammer. Be careful not to hit the beads—they'll break.

9 Repeat step 8 with the other wire.

10 String a cranberry bead, a blue bead, and a cranberry bead onto the wire.

11 To make the earring hooks, use the pliers to bend the unhammered wire into a U about ¹/2 inch away from the last loop. File the sharp edges off the tip with the metal file.

Squished Silver Necklace

Practice bending and hammering copper wire before you start working with sterling silver.

MATERIALS

Wire, 20 gauge (silver)

Wire, 24 gauge (silver)

Lobster-claw clasp and jump ring (silver)

TOOLS

Wire cutters

Round-nosed pliers

Piece of felt

Sidewalk

Hammer

WHAT YOU DO

1 Cut seven 4-inch-long pieces of 20-gauge wire with the wire cutters.

2 Bend loops and angles in each piece of wire with the round-nosed pliers. Use the pliers to make a loop in both ends of each piece of wire (see page 24).

figure 1

3 Set the pieces of wire on a piece of felt on the sidewalk. (The surface you hammer the wire on has to be really hard, and the felt will keep the texture of the sidewalk from transferring onto the wire.)

4 Use the hammer to pound the pieces of wire flat. Make sure you don't pound any one place too much, or the wire will break.

5 Set the hammered pieces of wire aside.

6 Cut eight ³/₄ inch-long pieces of 24-gauge wire.

7 Make a loop in one end of the first piece of wire. Make a loop going in the opposite direction close to the first loop and trim the excess wire. You now have a figure 8 (see figure 1).

8 Repeat step 7 until you've made all the pieces of wire into figure eights.

9 Arrange the hammered links in the order in which you want them.

10 Open one of the loops in a figure eight and attach it to the loop on the end of the first hammered link (see page 25). Close the loop.

11 Open the other loop in the figure eight and use it to attach the next hammered link.

12 Repeat steps 10 and 11 until you've linked all the hammered pieces.

13 Use the last two figure eights to attach the lobster-claw clasp and jump ring to the necklace.

Found Object Jewelry

How about a treasure hunt? The treasure you're seeking is cool stuff to turn into beads. Look around your house for interesting things to use. Anything that's got a hole in it is fair game. If it doesn't have a hole, see whether you can figure out how to make one. If you can't drill one, how about using the technique on page 54? Yard sales are also a great place to find old jewelry to take apart and remake into your own creations.

Found Object Jewelry

Junk Drawer Jewelry Choker

You can remake pieces of old jewelry into something brand new. Figure out how to attach all the pieces of jewelry to the ribbon before starting.

MATERIALS

Pieces of old jewelry

2 eye pins (silver)

2 end cones (silver)

2 jump rings (silver)

Lobster-claw clasp (silver)

Velvet ribbon, $7/8$ x $11^{1}/2$ inches (black)

Fine chain, 3 inches (silver)

TOOLS

Sewing needle and thread

Clear nail polish with nylon (see page 11)

Scissors

Round-nosed pliers

Wire cutters

Hot glue gun and glue sticks (optional)

WHAT YOU DO

1 Arrange the pieces of old jewelry on the ribbon. Make sure you know how you're going to attach each piece to the ribbon. You should be able to sew most of the pieces on—if you're desperate, you can use a hot glue gun. Don't attach the pieces yet.

2 Thread the needle with 7 inches of sewing thread. Tie a big knot in the end. Loosely stitch across one end of the ribbon, about $1/8$ inch from the edge (see figure 1).

3 Pull on the end of the thread so that the ribbon gathers together in a point. Take a few stitches through the gathered point to hold it securely in place.

4 Tie the end of the thread to one of the eye pins. Put a dab of nail polish on the knot. Cut off the excess thread with the scissors.

5 Pull the eye pin through the end cone. Make a loop in the end of the eye pin the round-nosed pliers (see page 24) and trim the excess wire with the wire cutters.

6 Repeat steps 3 through 5 on the other end of the ribbon.

7 Attach a jump ring to each end loop (see page 25). Attach the chain to one ring and the clasp to the other. Close the loops.

8 Attach the pieces of junk drawer jewelry to the velvet by sewing or gluing them.

figure 1

Copper Washer Bracelet

You can use the technique for linking the washers together on this bracelet but substitute stone donuts or Chinese coins instead.

MATERIALS

6 or 7 large copper washers (the number varies with the size of the washer used)

End coils

Lobster-claw clasp and jump ring (brass)

Leather cord, 1 mm (black)

Wire, 34 gauge (brass)

TOOLS

Scissors

Wire cutters

Cyanoacrylate glue*

Round-nosed pliers

*Available at craft stores (one brand is Superglue).

WHAT YOU DO

1 Cut a 10-inch-length of leather cord with the scissors. Cut a 10-inch-long piece of wire with the wire cutters.

2 Link two washers together with the cord by wrapping the cord through the center holes of the washers (see figure 1). Make three loose loops, being careful to keep the leather loops even and free from twists. Adjust the leather loops until the washers are about 1 inch apart.

3 Wrap the wire around the center of the leather loops. Wrap the wire several times, then twist the ends together tightly on the back of the bracelet to keep everything in place (see figure 1).

4 Trim the ends of the leather and the excess wire. Fold the remaining twisted wire over so that it is flat against the back of the bracelet.

5 Repeat steps 1 through 4 with the rest of the washers.

6 To attach the end coils, cut an 8-inch-long piece of leather cord. Wrap the leather around the last washer, using the same technique you did in step 2, but make only two loops.

7 Put a dab of glue on the end of the loops and push them into one of the end coils. With the needle-nosed pliers, crush the end of the coil around the threads (see page 30).

8 Repeat steps 6 and 7 on the other side.

9 Open the loop in one of the end coils to attach the clasp (see page 25). Close the loop. Repeat on the other side to attach the jump ring.

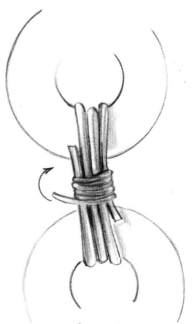

figure 1

Nuts & Bolts Necklace

This ultra-cool necklace will take some real hard wear!

WHAT YOU DO

1 Thread a nut, a washer, and a nut onto the ball chain.

2 Thread one of the resin beads and four nuts, with a washer in between each nut.

3 Thread a resin bead and six nuts, with a washer in between each nut.

4 Repeat step 3.

5 Repeat step 2.

6 Thread the last resin bead. Repeat step 1.

7 Add the ball chain connector to the ends of the ball chain.

The Oh-Wow, O-Ring Necklace

This awesome necklace uses rubber O-rings to hold the beads in place. You can find them at home improvement stores. Just make sure they're the right size to fit snugly on your cord.

MATERIALS

5 spiral beads from page 40

Polymer clay clasp from page 113

12 rubber O-rings (black)*

Rubber cord, 5mm (black)*

Cyanoacrylate glue**

TOOLS

Scissors

*Available at some bead and craft stores, and most home improvement stores

**Available at craft stores (one brand is Superglue)

WHAT YOU DO

1 Cut an 18-inch-long piece of rubber cord with the scissors.

2 Put a dab of glue on one end of the rubber cord. Stick it through the hole in the polymer clay clasp. Let it dry.

3 String an O-ring, a handmade bead, and another O-ring.

4 Slide the O-rings and the bead you just strung along the cord until they are about 4 inches away from the clasp.

5 Repeat step 3 and slide the O-rings and the bead until they are about 3/4 inch from the last bead.

6 Repeat steps 3, 4, and 5 until you've strung all the beads. You can slide the beads around on the cord until you're happy with the arrangement.

7 Slide the last two O-rings onto the cord. Make a loop in the end of the cord and hold it together with your fingers. Try pushing the polymer clay clasp through the loop. If the clasp falls out, make the loop smaller. If the clasp won't go through, make the loop bigger.

8 Trim the end of the cord at an angle, where the loop meets. Put a dab of glue on the cord and press it together, making the loop you measure in step 7. Roll the O-rings over the ends of the loop and let it dry.

Make These Beads!

Polymer Clay Toggle Clasp

Why search all over town for a clasp that will sort of match your necklace when you can make one that matches it perfectly?

MATERIALS

Polymer clay (to match your necklace)

TOOLS

Skewer

Cookie sheet

Oven

Oven mitts

WHAT YOU DO

1 Condition a small piece of the polymer clay (see Step 1 on page 40).

2 Roll the clay into a ball about ½ inch wide.

3 Poke a hole about halfway through the ball with the skewer. Don't poke all the way through.

4 Put the ball on the cookie sheet and bake it for 30 minutes according to the manufacturer's instructions. Remove the cookie sheet from the oven with the oven mitts. Let it cool completely.

5 Follow the instructions on page 110 to finish the clasp.

Monkeying Around Bracelet

I f you can't find the perfect charm at the bead store, make your own! Then use the instructions here to attach them to a charm bracelet.

MATERIALS

14 shrink-plastic charms from page 115

16 jump rings (silver)

Toggle clasp (silver)

Chain (silver)*

TOOLS

Wire cutter

Needle-nosed pliers

*Available at home improvement stores and some bead stores

WHAT YOU DO

1 With the wire cutters, cut the chain so it fits around your wrist. (See page 14 for hints on measuring.)

2 Arrange the charms along the length of the chain so you'll know how far apart to space them. (They're spaced 1 inch apart in our bracelet.)

3 Open a jump ring with the needle-nosed pliers (see page 25).

4 String a charm onto the jump ring. Thread the jump ring through the chain and close it.

5 Repeat steps 3 and 4 until you've used up all the charms, using the spacing you determined in step 2.

6 Attach the clasp to the bracelet with jump rings.

Make These Beads!

Shrink-Plastic Charms

You can put just about ANYTHING on shrink plastic. Draw your own designs directly onto the rough side of the shrink plastic or trace an image you like onto it. Then, watch the plastic shrink in the oven.

MATERIALS

2 sheets of plain white paper

Clear shrink plastic*

TOOLS

Monkey stamp

Inkpad

Palm tree stamp

Photocopier

Brown- and green-colored pencils

Brown, yellow, and green markers

Scissors

Small hole punch

Oven

Cookie sheet

Aluminum foil

Small butter knife (optional)

Oven mitts

*Available at craft stores

WHAT YOU DO

1 Press the monkey stamp into the inkpad. Press the monkey stamp onto a sheet of plain white paper.

2 Press the palm tree stamp into the inkpad. Press the stamp onto a second sheet of plain white paper.

3 Using a photocopier, reduce the monkey image by 25 percent. Reduce the palm tree image by 50 percent.

4 Place a sheet of clear shrink plastic (rough side up) on top of the monkey image. Use the brown-colored pencil to trace the monkey image onto the shrink plastic. Color the monkey with the brown and yellow markers. Repeat six times, then carefully cut out all the monkeys.

5 Place a sheet of clear shrink plastic (rough side up) on top of the palm tree image. Use the brown and green colored pencils to trace the palm tree image onto the shrink plastic. Color the palm tree with the brown and green markers. Repeat six times, then carefully cut out all the palm trees.

6 Punch holes in the tops of all the prepared charms before baking.

7 Preheat the oven to 275°F. Cover a cookie sheet with aluminum foil. Place all the charms rough side up on the cookie sheet.

8 Place the cookie sheet in the oven. Watch the charms as they melt. The plastic will curl and bend as it shrinks. If it sticks, use a small butter knife to separate it, then continue shrinking. The plastic will begin to flatten out. After the plastic is flat, count to 30, then remove the cookie sheet from the oven using the oven mits. The whole process takes 1 to 2 minutes. Let the charms cool.

Fossil Necklace

Y ou can make a graduated necklace out of any kind of bead that changes size. The "beads" in this project are **crinoids**, the fossilized bodies of ancient marine critters.

EXPERT ADVICE

⟲ String this necklace from the middle if you're not sure whether you have enough beads. Start with the biggest bead and center it in the middle. Then work on both sides at once. Be careful not to drop the ends! If you don't have enough graduated beads, use filler beads to make your necklace the right length (see page 37).

MATERIALS

Different-sized tube beads

Seed beads, 8° (matte transparent green)

2 crimp beads (silver)

Toggle clasp (silver)

Nylon-coated beading wire

TOOLS

Piece of cloth

Wire cutters

Needle-nosed pliers

WHAT YOU DO

1 Lay the piece of cloth on your work surface and put the beads on it. (The cloth will keep them from rolling away.) Arrange the beads in a line so that the smallest beads are on either end and the largest bead is in the middle.

2 Cut a 20-inch length of beading wire with the wire cutters. String one crimp bead and one end of the toggle clasp. Go back through the crimp bead and squish it with the needle-nosed pliers (see page 29).

3 String one green seed bead and the smallest graduated bead.

4 Continue alternating a green bead and a graduated bead until you've strung enough beads to go around your neck.

5 String one crimp bead and the other end of the toggle clasp. Go back through the crimp bead and squish it. Trim the excess wire.

Cute-as-a-Button Toe Rings

Teeny toe rings are the perfect way to use all those mismatched buttons your grandmother has been hoarding.

MATERIALS

Small button

Beading elastic, 0.5mm (black)

TOOLS

Scissors

WHAT YOU DO

1 Cut a 6-inch-long piece of elastic with the scissors.

2 Thread the elastic through one of the holes in the back of the button. Go through the other hole in the button.

3 Wrap the ring around your toe to measure it. It should be snug enough to stay on without flopping around, but not so tight that it stretches out the elastic.

4 Tie a square knot in the end of the elastic (see page 31) and trim the excess elastic.

Flowery Ribbon Chokers

Possibly the simplest, fastest, easiest project in this book, these chokers are so fun to make that you'll want a whole garden full!

MATERIALS

Whatever you want to put on the choker (ribbons, fake flowers, pearls, beads, etc.)

2 snaps

Fusible fabric interfacing*

Two different types of ribbon, one wider than the other

TOOLS

Scissors

Iron

Hot glue gun and glue sticks

Pencil

Sewing needle and thread

*Available at sewing and craft stores

WHAT YOU DO

1 With the scissors, cut the wider ribbon so it fits around your neck with ¹/₂ inch overlap, (see page 14 for measuring tips).

2 Cut the thinner ribbon the same length as the wider ribbon. Position it on top of the wider ribbon.

3 Cut the fusible interfacing so it is slightly smaller than the thinner ribbon. Put it between the two pieces of ribbon and fuse the two pieces together with the iron.

4 Arrange your decorations in the center of the ribbon. When you're happy with the arrangement, glue them to the ribbon with the hot glue gun.

5 Let the glue dry. Then, put on the choker and use a pencil to mark where the snaps should go. You want one on the top and one on the bottom of each end. The choker should fit snugly, but not so tight that it chokes you.

6 Thread the sewing needle with the thread and stitch the snaps into place. Make sure you sew the front half of a snap to one end of the ribbon and the back half to the other end so that they'll snap.

Foam Cuffs

Y ou can make a foam cuff in a matter of moments—perfect for that last-minute party gift!

MATERIALS

Whatever you want to put on the cuff (ribbons, fake fur, plastic or lace flowers, sequins, beads, etc.)

Craft foam

Hook and loop tape*

TOOLS

Scissors

Pencil

Hot glue gun and glue sticks

*Available at craft stores (one brand is Velcro)

WHAT YOU DO

1 With the scissors, cut the craft foam so that it overlaps your wrist by 1 inch (see page 14 for measuring tips).

2 Arrange your decorations on the cuff until you like the way it looks. Mark their placement with the pencil.

3 Use the hot glue gun to glue your decorations to the cuff. Start with the bottom layer of stuff. Let the glue dry between each layer.

4 Cut the hook and loop tape into two small pieces. Position it on the ends of the bracelet so it will hold it together. Remember, one half has to be on the bottom of the bracelet and the other half will be on the top of the bracelet.

5 If you have self-adhesive hook and loop tape, just pull off the protective backing and stick it in place. If you don't, use the hot glue gun to glue it into place.

Templates

Zuni Bear Pendant

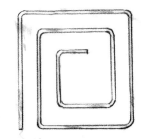

Wire Rectangle Paper Clip

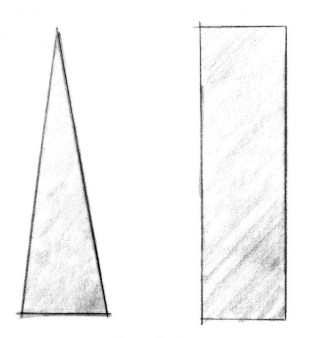

Paper Beads

Metric Conversions

$1/8$ inch	=	3mm
$1/4$ inch	=	6mm
$1/2$ inch	=	1.3 cm
$3/4$ inch	=	1.9 cm
1 inch	=	2.5 cm
2 inches	=	5.1 cm
3 inches	=	7.6 cm
4 inches	=	10.2 cm
5 inches	=	12.7 cm
6 inches	=	15.2 cm
7 inches	=	17.8 cm
8 inches	=	20.3 cm
9 inches	=	22.9 cm
10 inches	=	25.4 cm
11 inches	=	27.9 cm
12 inches	=	30.5 cm
13 inches	=	33 cm
14 inches	=	35.6 cm
15 inches	=	38.1 cm
16 inches	=	40.6 cm

17 inches	=	43.2 cm
18 inches	=	45.7 cm
19 inches	=	48.3 cm
20 inches	=	50.8 cm
21 inches	=	53.3 cm
22 inches	=	55.9 cm
23 inches	=	58.2 cm
24 inches	=	61 cm
25 inches	=	63.5 cm
26 inches	=	66 cm
27 inches	=	68.6 cm
28 inches	=	71.1 cm
29 inches	=	73.7 cm
30 inches	=	76.2 cm
40 inches	=	101.6 cm
60 inches	=	152.4 cm
1 yard	=	0.9 m
2 yards	=	1.8 m
4 yards	=	3.6 m

Designers

Special thanks to the
talented team of
designers who created
the projects in this book:

IRENE DEAN

has been doing amazing things with polymer clay since 1992. She is the author of *Kids' Crafts: Polymer Clay* (Lark Books, 2003) as well as a whole bunch of other great books on polymer clay. She lives in the mountains of Western North Carolina. Her projects are on pages 39, 43, and 112.

DIANA LIGHT

has an uncanny ability to turn the most ordinary objects into extraordinary works of art, simply by adding a little of this and a little of that. Everything she touches turns into something cool! Her projects are on pages 38, 46, 50, 52, 56, 71, 72, 89, 93, 103, and 108.

MARTHE LE VAN

never leaves her house without an astonishing array of jewelry. She can wear earrings, a necklace, several bracelets, and up to 10 rings all at the same time! (Let her example be your inspiration.) She lives in Asheville, NC. Her projects appear on pages 118 and 119.

ALLISON CHANDLER SMITH

lives in Asheville, NC. In addition to operating an interior redesign business, she works as a freelance crafter, writer, and designer. She is the author of *The Girls' World Book of Bath & Beauty* (Lark Books, 2004). She made the projects on pages 44, 51, 60, 61, 76, 101, 110, 114, and 117.

TERRY TAYLOR

artist and crafter extraordinaire, made several great projects for this book. In his spare time, he makes stunning jewelry with the help of soldering irons, blow torches, and those sorts of thing. The "low-tech" projects he designed for this book appear on pages 41, 66, 95, and 111.

KATHRYN TEMPLE

is a celebrated visual artist who exhibits and sells her paintings and other artworks throughout the country. She teaches art to middle school students and is the author of a forthcoming kid's book about drawing (Lark Books, 2005). She lives in Asheville, NC, with her dog Sadie and her cat Mouse. Her projects are on pages 53, 55, 62-63, 67, 70, 73, 74, 92, 94, 97, 100, 104, and 105.

I made the projects on pages 36, 37, 80, 81, 84, 86, 88, and 116.

Hey Kids!

What did you think of
this book?
We want to hear all
about it.
Send us an e mail at
kids@larkbooks.com,
or send us some snail
mail at:
Kids at Lark
Lark Books
67 Broadway
Asheville, NC, 28801

Our Models

Jasmine

Leila

Alex

India

Anna

Cierra

Daniela

Hana

Sarah

Lacey

Oliana

Olivia

Pearl

Lydia

Adelyn

Skye

Sharnel

Index